Praise for *White Devil*

"Bob Halloran's *White Devil* opens with a bang and doesn't let up. Halloran's in-your-face narrative, honest and straightforward, packs power and punch, not to mention the elegance and integrity of old-school, gumshoe reporting. The book is daring and dangerous, full of that gritty, no-nonsense, take-no-prisoners storytelling found in any classic Boston crime book. Open *White Devil* and enter the hell Halloran has created with this incredible, haunting read."

—M. WILLIAM PHELPS,
New York Times bestselling author

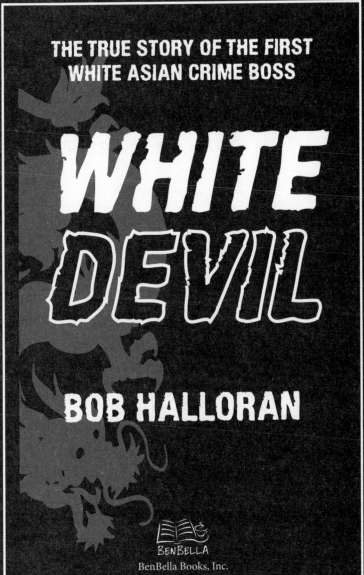

THE TRUE STORY OF THE FIRST
WHITE ASIAN CRIME BOSS

WHITE
DEVIL

BOB HALLORAN

BenBella

BenBella Books, Inc.
Dallas, Texas

The events, locations, and conversations in this book, while true, are recreated from the author's memory. However, the essence of the story, and the feelings and emotions evoked, are intended to be accurate representations. In certain instances, names, persons, organizations, and places have been changed to protect an individual's privacy.

BenBella Books, Inc.
10300 N. Central Expressway
Suite #530
Dallas, TX 75231
www.benbellabooks.com
Send feedback to feedback@benbellabooks.com

Printed in the United States of America
10 9 8 7 6 5 4 3 2 1

Library of Congress Cataloging-in-Publication Data

Halloran, Bob, author.
    White devil : the true story of the first white Asian crime boss / Bob Halloran.
        pages cm
    Includes bibliographical references and index.
    ISBN 978-1-940363-79-0 (trade cloth : alk. paper) — ISBN 978-1-940363-89-9 (electronic) 1.
Gangsters—Massachusetts—Boston—Biography. 2. Organized crime—Massachussetts—Boston. 3.
Chinatown (Boston, Mass.)—Social conditions. 4. Willis, John, 1971- I. Title.
    HV6452.M4H35 2016
    364.1092—dc23
    [B]

                                                                                        2015030748

Editing by Erin Kelley
Copyediting by Karen Levy
Proofreading by Michael Fedison and Lisa Story
Cover design and illustration by Rodrigo Corral Design
Jacket design by Sarah Dombrowsky
Text design and composition by John Reinhardt Book Design
Printed by Lake Book Manufacturing

Distributed by Perseus Distribution
www.perseusdistribution.com

To place orders through Perseus Distribution:
Tel: (800) 343-4499
Fax: (800) 351-5073
E-mail: orderentry@perseusbooks.com

Significant discounts for bulk sales are available.
Please contact Aida Herrera at aida@benbellabooks.com.

A dedication with devotion to my lovely wife, Eileen.

Years of love have come and gone, and many more will follow.

CONTENTS

INTRODUCTION

I MET JOHN WILLIS at FCI Cumberland, a medium-security federal prison in Cumberland, Maryland, in the winter of 2014. After being cleared through security, I was taken to a small room with a table and two chairs. I sat with my back to the window overlooking the prison yard and facing the visitors' room where several families spent time with dozens of inmates. It was a casual atmosphere with children playing and guards providing plenty of freedom to mingle.

After a few minutes, John walked in unaccompanied by a guard. He wore an orange jumpsuit, and he wasn't handcuffed. I don't think I expected him to be restrained, but I found myself surprised to be left alone in a room with a criminal known to have a violent past. I stood up and John shook my hand with a friendly greeting. And then we talked for three hours.

He was at all times engaging, charming, and clearly intelligent. He was never intimidating. His voice stayed low and under control. He didn't smile often, but there wasn't a lot of humor in our conversation. He wanted to tell his story, and he knew I was the person who would tell it. I think he was honest about everything he said, though there were some things he was reluctant to discuss.

For instance, I thought it was interesting when I asked him if he had ever killed anyone, and he smiled a little, and said: "I can't answer that."

"Well, if you asked me that question," I responded, "I could answer it. It would be easy. I'd say, 'No.'"

I don't know if John's nonresponsiveness means that he has committed murder, or if he just wanted me to think that he might have. I think he's fond of his reputation as a tough guy, and sees the benefits of people thinking he's capable of murder.

In any event, I liked my time with John. We spent three hours the first day and four more the second. I grew very comfortable with him as we debated religion, God, philosophy, honor codes, self-determination, self-preservation, and the Boston Red Sox.

I drove away with seven hours of recorded conversation, all of which would be transcribed for accurate quotes, and all the information John gave me would need to be corroborated by other witnesses, investigators, wiretaps, federal or criminal court documents, and newspaper accounts. I also had several hours of transcribed interviews from my manager, Matt Valentinas, conducted separately with John and his girlfriend, Anh Nguyen. That information, along with my own interview with Anh, formed the basis of a lengthy research process that included additional interviews with members of John's family, social circle, one former gang member, and the FBI.

A wealth of information and detail came directly from the first and second superceding indictments in which a grand jury charged John and several others with drug trafficking and money laundering—charges to which John and most of his associates pleaded guilty. Those indictments included transcribed phone conversations recorded by legal wiretaps. They also confirmed and added details to John's version of money seizures, drug buys, and his own purchases of luxury items such as boats, cars, and houses—all of which were cited in the money laundering charges against him.

Affidavits submitted by FBI Special Agent Timothy C. McElroy for the continued use of electronic surveillance and by FBI Special Agent Thomas Conboy in support of the government's motion to detain certain defendants clearly laid out the case against John and his coconspirators, and led to court-approved wiretaps of nine targeted telephones for nearly six months. Three of those phones were John's. And you will read excerpts of what investigators recorded.

The FBI built a case against John and more than two dozen others that included narcotics distribution, money laundering, illegal gambling, extortion, alien smuggling, racketeering, human trafficking, and prostitution. Only one accomplice, Colby Deering, took his case to court. The trial transcripts with several coconspirators testifying under oath further corroborated or illuminated my research.

There were several reports in the *Quincy Patriot Ledger,* the *San Francisco Weekly,* the *San Francisco Chronicle,* the *Boston Globe,* and the *New York Times* from which I used information, eyewitness accounts, and quotes. Those are not footnoted in the book for the purpose of fluid reading, but I acknowledge them here.

What I learned from combining John's stories with diligent research was that John had been honest, though a bit fuzzy on details and names. For instance, when John told me about a friend of his being killed right in front of him in a parking lot, this is what he said:

"His name was Wing. He had just gotten out of prison for robbing jewelry stores in Lowell. I knew him when he got out. It would be 1994–95."

Well, as it turns out, a man named Chay Giang was killed in that parking lot under the same circumstances John described, but it happened in 1991.

John simply knew Chay Giang as Wing the same way he new his own boss as Bai Ming, even though Bai Ming also went by Bike Ming, and his real name is Tan Ngo. Another criminal convicted under the name Truong Chi Trung was known by many as either Ah Sing or Ay-yat. John refers to him as Pida; although for quite a while I thought he was saying "Peter." Clarifying all the aliases and discovering that many Asian gang members used Americanized names like

Kevin or William was one of the more difficult challenges in assuring the information in this book is accurate.

Some names have been changed to protect the privacy of some individuals, but I offer a good-faith assurance that all other information is factual.

ONE

T WAS COLLECTION DAY, and all the aging Chinese men who ran the dozens of low-stakes gambling dens and popular restaurants in Boston's Chinatown were prepared to pay that month's extortion money. The envelopes full of cash were usually transferred with a broad smile that belied each victim's begrudging nature. They no longer felt the fear of what would happen if they didn't pay, because they always paid. So the fear was gone, long since replaced by something far worse—a weekly emasculation at the hands of an abnormally large white guy who had them by the balls.

"I was always polite," John Willis says reassuringly. "My boss, Bai Ming, would send me, and he always said when you go to collect money, make them respect you. Sometimes you'd have a problem. You'd have to, you know, do damage. Whether it's beating people up, or sometimes you might put their hand on the grill; do something to really get the point across."

John began collecting for Bai Ming as a teenager in the late 1980s. The first time he ran into a problem was at a gambling den on Harrison Avenue. He went in and introduced himself to the owner, and told him he was collecting for Ming. The owner was as surprised as he was offended that a round-eyed white kid would enter his place of business and demand money.

"Who does this white boy think he is?" the owner said to another man in Chinese. "He should just leave and go fuck his mother."

The two men continued speaking in Chinese, mocking John and laughing. John stood patiently for a moment before turning around and locking the door. He then proceeded to tear the place apart. He turned over tables, smashed chairs, and pulled the lights down from the ceiling. When he was done and the gambling den looked like a disaster area, John walked up to the owner and spoke softly but firmly to him in perfect Chinese.

"Next time just give me the money. Don't insult me. Don't disrespect me, and don't make me go through this again, or it won't be furniture I break. Understand?"

"Oh, you speak Chinesey," the owner said, managing a smile.

"No, I don't speak Chinesey," John corrected him. "I speak Chinese. Now, go fuck your mother."

JOHN WILLIS SMILED at the memory and inhaled deeply. Willis is a large, muscular man of English, Portuguese, and Cherokee Indian descent, made even larger by persistent steroid use. He keeps his hair cropped short in a neat and stylish crew cut. His eyes are blue. His face is round and handsome. He is much too serious to allow for a broad, carefree smile. Laughter is a luxury. He is all business all the time.

His moment of fond reminiscing ended abruptly when he heard the distinctive echo that can only be made when metal doors are slammed shut. He listened to the muffled whimpers of strong men crying into their pillows. Moments later the lights were turned out, and he felt the loneliness that darkness brings. He sensed fear all around him, and as he felt it growing inside of himself, he jumped down to the cold cement floor and he prayed.

John forced his large, muscular body into a modified lotus position, closed his eyes, and listened to his own heartbeat. He concentrated solely on its rhythm until the space between beats grew remarkably wide, and his breathing was shallow enough to be imperceptible. He pushed out thoughts of anger and self-pity, and wrestled with the self-awareness that caused him to both love and loathe himself. Finally reaching a more peaceful state, John thought about all the people he loved in his life. There were exactly two—his wife and his daughter. Prior to meeting his wife, Anh Nguyen, he had no familiarity with either love or fear, and the sudden appearance of both disrupted his core beliefs. Love and fear threatened his way of life. They made him vulnerable in ways that could get him killed, and he felt love, in particular, weakening him every day. It must be love, he thought, "because it brings a lot of pain." His mind didn't land on the notion that love brings a lot of happiness. There's far too much conflict and guilt and rising thoughts of violence associated with love for it to ever offer John the false hope of pure joy. Love was far more likely to fuel his rage.

"Somebody hit my wife one time in a nightclub," John recalled. "I was in New York, and somebody called me and told me. They've never seen that guy again. And nobody ever will. He shouldn't have put his hands on her. The fact of the matter is the guy will never, ever do that again. Whoever knew about it, or was involved in it, they were getting whatever he was getting. When it comes to my wife, I'm not arguing. I don't have a problem with taking out five or six guys just to get to the right one. Then it's over. And I sleep a little better."

The memory of having done the right thing helped John relax. He continued rubbing his thumb and forefinger gently, smoothly, and continuously for nearly an hour, and he thought only about his wife and daughter.

"May they be well, happy, and peaceful," he said over and over.

John was so entranced by his meditative state, so singularly focused on his purpose, that he was able to achieve a serenity that stood in stark contrast to his surroundings. John Willis was quietly celebrating his forty-second birthday in jail. He would certainly celebrate his forty-third, and there could be as many as eighteen birthdays after that spent behind bars.

Before rising from the floor, John took a moment to recognize the circuitous nature of his life's journey. Sitting on the cold jail floor, alone and praying, was notably similar to when John was fifteen years old and convinced he would die on his kitchen floor. He was cold, hungry, and alone then, too.

"I wasn't looking to do anything other than survive as a kid," John says. "I went from surviving to basically taking everything I wanted. The way I look at it, there's a lot taken for granted in this country. You go home, you shut your door, you're inside, you have heat, you eat food, and you live there. But what happens when I'm a kid and my mom dies? There's no more food, there's no more heat. Now there's a need to survive. I wanted to actually make something of my life. In the beginning, I was angry at the world, very angry that my mother had passed away and I was in a situation with no money. No nothing. I didn't have family, because my sisters were caught up in drugs. I was basically taken in by a family who was Chinese. I grew up just a whole different species than what was around me. I found myself in a society that didn't trust anybody, never mind somebody white, somebody American. And then to be given duty, honor, and respect—to me that was something I cherished, and to this day I do."

What John offers there is a stripped-down summary of his life that attempts to explain why he chose an amoral, greedy, and violent path, but never broaches why he rejected an infinite number of alternate routes. His circumstances, dire as they were, taught him lessons that some would affirm and others would renounce. But from the time he was a boy, John Willis was convinced he knew what it meant to be a man. He was taught that a man is a soldier. And nothing more.

Willis didn't fight on a traditional battlefield. He fought in the streets, and the enemy was constantly changing. Willis' enemies were from rival gangs or the local police. Both were out to get him. There were the businessmen he robbed, and the victims he bludgeoned. All sought vengeance. There were prostitutes and gamblers, drug dealers and drug users, and countless others who would have loved to see John Willis taken down or taken out. But Willis survived it all. And what's the point of surviving, if you're not going to live a little? That's why, despite his own best advice and against his own self-interest, he bought a Porsche, a Bentley, and a multimillion-dollar home. Those purchases were self-destructive, but they made him feel good. He knew the police took notice of a gangster flashing lots of cash, but like an addict, Willis needed to feel good, if only temporarily. Those purchases were not only his drug; they were evidence of his righteous pursuits. He was winning the war, so God must be on his side.

"I believe that God loves me," Willis says with conviction, but anticipates his faith may be met with doubt, and adds, "You might say, 'How could God love me?' Well, if he doesn't love me, he doesn't give me anything. Some people he puts to the test. I'm all about the test. I really do think God loves me, and I love people. I'm not a monster. I love people, and I have a value for each and every person. But I also believe if you're a person deserving of what you get, that's what you get. That's how it goes."

And in John Willis' world, he decides what a person deserves. For instance, the man in the Chinese restaurant who once brazenly told John to "shut the fuck up" deserved to be struck with an open hand and hit over the head with a Glock pistol. So, John did those things.

"And then I stuck the gun in his eye," John continues. "He's bleeding. People are looking at me and they're scared. They took the guy into the bathroom and cleaned him up. For me it was nothing. He was no one. I turned, and had a drink with everybody. I thank God the man left, because I might have gone back in the alley and shot him. When I go back to the bar, I'm not shaking. I'm thinking—where do I want this to go? Did I go too far, or did I not go far enough?"

Such is the mentality of a street soldier. John is convinced now more than ever that a man fights every day for his own survival. A man is a self-centered creature who recognizes that contentment, like true happiness, is not only unattainable; it is the foolish pursuit of the embattled and desperate losers of the war. John Willis is a man. He lives these principles unwaveringly. He is a soldier who believes he is fighting the good fight, and that he is winning the war. Shedding his white skin, adopting a culture he was not born into, and surviving into his forties is proof of that, and surviving remains the greatest accomplishment of the man his enemies call the White Devil.

JOHN WILLIS was born May 11, 1971, at Boston City Hospital. He was brought home to a three-family house at 37 South Munroe Terrace in Dorchester. His father, an ex-con who worked as a carpenter, was a large, angry man who drank too much and beat his wife, Francine. When he ultimately ran afoul of the Irish Mob, he escaped to an Indian reservation in the mountains of South Carolina. It was better for everyone that he left, but John, who was only three years old at the time, grew to hate a father he never really knew.

So, John was raised by his mother, Francine, and her three much older children from a previous marriage. John's brother, Richie, who owned the home and lived on the second floor with his wife and three daughters, took on paternal responsibilities. He helped with the bills and administered strict discipline. Richie was a hardworking man who built a successful carpet business. He had two passions: fishing on his large boat, and drugs. John says Richie did a line of cocaine every night when he came home from work.

John's last memory of his brother is when Richie forcefully threw him down the stairs.

"I wish you were dead!" John cried out.

Two days later, Richie died of a heart attack brought on by his cocaine addiction. He was thirty-four years old.

"That really messed me up," John recalls now.

Richie's death caused Francine to go into a yearlong depression. She continued to do the best she could to make John happy. In fact, she spoiled John. Making good money as an executive at the Stride Rite shoe factory in nearby Roxbury, Francine lavished John with the best of everything. He had the finest shoes and clothes, the latest toys, and his hockey equipment was the envy of his blue-collar neighborhood friends. Suddenly, it all went away.

Perhaps if Francine had complained sooner about the pain in her calves and thighs, things would have been different, but a year after Richie's death, Francine suffered complications from her diabetes.

"She went in for open heart surgery, and they took her legs," John's cousin Debbie recalls. "Gangrene had set in. She was a very, very pretty woman. A beautiful mix of Italian and Indian. She looked like Liz Taylor. But when they took her legs, that's when everything went downhill."

Francine's depression grew worse. Her self-image was shattered. She was given big, heavy prosthetic legs that she lacked the strength to maneuver. She was an invalid left in the care of a fourteen-year-old boy.

"I think it was at this point that my life and my view of it changed," John considers aloud. "I was mad at God and the whole world for bringing so much pain to my life."

John's sisters, Sandra and Linda, who were eighteen and sixteen years older than John, respectively, were busy with their own growing families. They thought Richie's widow, Sonny, who still lived upstairs, was helping to take care of things, and she thought the sisters were, but it all fell upon John's shoulders. He was left alone to cook, to clean, to shop, to give his mother her insulin shots, and to get her to the bathroom for showers and all other purposes. It was humiliating for both of them.

John loved his mother and did his best for her, but he was helpless when it came to her weakening heart and her overwhelming sorrow. Those things took her independence, her will, and ultimately her life. Francine Willis was taken to Mount Sinai Hospital in Stoughton for additional care and rehab, but she died there. John was effectively an orphan at fifteen.

"He was extremely angry," Debbie recalls. "That's when the anger started. That's when he stopped being Johnny. He started being something else."

John never cried over his mother's death, and he didn't talk to anyone about it. He received no consolation from his sisters. In fact, the only conversation he had with Linda was at the wake when he scolded her and accused her of being stoned. He was only at the wake for ten minutes before he stormed out, and he didn't attend his mother's funeral.

That is the line of demarcation in John's life. There was the time before his mother's illness and death, and the time after. His life, his mood, and especially his path were forever altered. The spoiled, happy-go-lucky kid from the neighborhood had been transformed. The boy had prematurely become a man, and that meant fifteen-year-old John Willis was a soldier. From the day his mother died, he was ready for a fight. He'd fight any kid in the neighborhood and beat him senseless without fear of repercussion. He fought for survival.

He fought back tears and sorrow, and even joy, and every emotion that began to scratch the surface. But his demons? Those he chose not to fight. His demons ran free.

Under normal circumstances, John would have been sent to live with either of his two sisters. He'd continue going to high school and upon graduation, he'd either find a job or go on to college. Other kids have endured greater hardships and gone on to live successful, respectable lives. But there was nothing normal about John's circumstances.

First, no one wanted John. There was no family member, no teacher, no hockey coach, no Department of Child Services that reached out to help. He lived for a while at Linda's apartment on Branch Street in Quincy with her husband, Vinny, and their children, but he was clearly not welcomed there. The apartment was too crowded, and the parties were wild. So John returned to live alone on the first floor of the house he'd shared with his mother.

Left to pay his own way, he dropped out of school and took a job with Vinny installing windows. He lived on a steady diet of Burger King hamburgers and fries, and steroids. He got the food from Debbie, who worked at Burger King, and he got the steroids from a couple of guys at the Universal Gym in North Quincy. He went from being a chubby kid to a ripped bodybuilder pretty quickly. Those who knew he was on steroids assumed the drugs were the cause of his abrupt and angry outbursts. They didn't understand his rage went much deeper than that.

John survived that way for a year until Brant Welty, a close friend, told him he could get work as a bouncer if he said he was seventeen. John referred to him as his brother. They had known each other since elementary school, but after John's mother passed, Brant's family had welcomed John into their home as often as they could. John would never forget that kindness.

Brant had always been a good kid. As a seven-year-old, he washed car windows in Kenmore Square outside Fenway Park. He was a straight "A" student in elementary and middle school, and his employment record included time at Burger King, a Greyhound bus station, and his father's watch and jewelry store in the Back Bay. Brant excelled in high school at Boston English in Jamaica Plain, and was offered a scholarship to Dartmouth College, but opted instead to become a jeweler like his father.

Meanwhile, John took a job as a bouncer at Narcissus, a Kenmore Square nightclub in Boston. The manager of the club, John Pop, didn't know or care that John was only sixteen. The club needed bouncers who were unusually large, barrel-chested, and muscular, and John fit the description. They also liked the anger and fearlessness emanating from John's eyes.

John took his job seriously. He ignored the loud music and the pretty college girls, and simply stood with his arms folded across his chest. John had been warned that the Asian gang kids from nearby Chinatown could be ruthless and violent, but his nervousness around them dissipated with each encounter, and he came to respect their excessive politeness. He was also envious of the expensive clothes they wore, the fancy cars they drove, and the money they flashed.

"All the things I want out of life," John thought.

One night, a fight broke out between a group of preppy college kids and a young Chinese man named Woping Joe. John knocked one of the assailants out cold, but not before Woping Joe had been maced.

"So, I took Woping Joe to the back and began helping him rinse his face," John said. "I turned to get some help and stared at six pissed-off-looking gangsters."

The gangsters were late coming to Woping Joe's rescue and assumed John needed a good beating, or worse. John stood his ground. His eyes darted from one face to another. There was a lot of indecipherable shouting in broken English, but he clearly heard the word "kill" several times, and he noticed the group had more than one gun and several knives.

"He cool," Woping Joe loudly repeated several times, and after a brief discussion in Cantonese, Woping Joe was able to convince the small mob to file out of the bathroom. Woping Joe turned back and handed John a card with a number on it.

"Hey, white boy," he said with a smile. "Here's a number to call."

John didn't know why he saved the number, but as another bitter winter descended upon New England, he would soon discover it was a fortuitous decision. When he was unable to pay the heat or electric bills on a bouncer's wages, his sister-in-law, Sonny, shut off the utilities on the first floor. John routinely came home from work, wrapped himself up tightly in a blanket, and lay down on his kitchen floor. He was sixteen years old, freezing cold, hungry, and alone in the dark.

One night in January of 1987, while the snow piled up outside his door, John felt the fear, anger, and frustration of his predicament overwhelm him. He curled into a fetal position and wondered how death would come to him. Would he slowly starve over a matter of days, or would he mercifully be taken in the night as he slept and froze to death?

Once he managed to shake off his moment of self-pity, John rose from the floor, bundled himself up in most of the clothes he owned, and walked through a snowstorm to a pay phone. He called his sister Sandra, who lived several towns over in Braintree with their grandparents and her three children. Sandra assured John that he could stay with them for a while, but after John used his last twenty dollars on cab fare, he arrived to find that Sandra wouldn't open the door for him.

John slumped his shoulders and put his hands in his pockets. Out of one he pulled three quarters and a penny. From the other, he found the card with the phone number on it from Woping Joe.

"What other choice do I have?" he thought to himself.

In truth, if he had thought longer, or if he was guided less by anger and self-pity, he might have considered his aunt and uncle, Debbie's parents. His aunt had been married several times and moved around a bit, and his uncle had moved back to South Carolina when his kids were grown. So, both of them would have taken some effort to locate, but John didn't even try, nor did he reach out to Debbie, who was three years older, putting herself through school, and living in Chelsea.

"Could I have taken him in?" Debbie wonders now. "Could I have supported him? I don't know, but I would have tried like hell. I would have made sure he wasn't hungry and that he went back to school. Maybe I didn't reach out to him. There were a number of people who could have helped. Sonny and his sisters threw him away like he was trash."

John traipsed back through the snow and went looking for a second pay phone. He remembered why and when he had been given the phone number, but he didn't really know what it was for, or who would pick up on the other end when he called. But as he fought the wind and the snow and walked several miles from Braintree to Quincy, he gripped the card tightly in his hand and did something he hadn't done in a long time. He hoped.

The real beginning for John was that snowy January night in 1987 when he reached a phone booth on Furnace Brook Parkway in Quincy, unclenched his fist, and stared at the crumpled card with only a ten-digit number on it. With fingers numb from the cold, John dropped one of his last quarters into the coin slot and slowly dialed the rotary phone. After the third ring, Woping Joe answered.

"*Ni hao*," Woping Joe said.

John had picked up a few Chinese words while working at the bar, and he recognized the greeting as the Chinese word for "hello."

"*Ni hao*," he replied with an inherent South Boston accent that revealed his identity.

"Hey," Woping Joe said, "you're the white boy from the bar. What do you want?"

John explained the predicament he was in, and to his astonishment, Woping Joe told him someone would be by in ten minutes to pick him up. John waited inside the phone booth where it was still freezing, but at least it was dry and the wind wasn't cutting through the hole in his jacket. Tragedy had hardened him so much that John had forgotten how to feel scared. So, ten minutes later, when two cars, a brand-new Acura and a BMW, rolled up on him, and a Chinese stranger said, "Get in," John got in without hesitation.

He was taken to a large three-family house in Braintree where he was immediately surrounded by more than a dozen Asian gangsters. Most of them only glanced up at the white boy in their midst. Others stared him down. John stood nervously in the middle of the room. He noticed each of the gangsters had a gun tucked into his waistband. He saw the latest electronics. He heard music blaring from an expensive stereo, and he smelled a delicious aroma he'd later learn was Chinese noodles. It was a sensory overload that should have made John turn and run, but it didn't.

"It was so badass!" John remembers. "I loved it!"

Several Asian women came out of the kitchen and were told by the men to serve dinner and set another place. John struggled to use chopsticks, which brought about plenty of laughter at the table, and that laughter only grew when John surrendered, picked up his bowl, and shoveled the food into his mouth with his thick fingers. The gangsters followed suit and good-naturedly copied John, who couldn't help but laugh himself. It was a fun-filled family dinner like John had never experienced. He looked around the room and saw faces quite unlike his own, and yet he felt at home. He couldn't know at the time that the seeds had just been planted for something that would grow strong inside him. Those were the seeds of loyalty and respect, and they would be nurtured over time. They were the seeds of an easier way. Never again would John face difficult decisions about right or wrong. If someone gave him respect, he returned it. If someone failed to show him respect, he showed that person what a mistake that was. There was a surprising simplicity in honor. And John would find weeding out the complexities of conscience or societal norms made it easy to accept otherwise unacceptable behavior.

"I can never say enough about these people," John says sincerely. "As far as being family oriented, your brother is your brother, you know? Things are just the way they are. You don't ask questions. It is what it is. To be taught a different culture, to live that culture, and to experience things that I have experienced, I have no regrets for anything that happened to me."

John sat at the Asian gangsters' dinner table that first night unaware that the direction of his life had been permanently and irreversibly altered. Unwittingly, Woping Joe had just become the catalyst for everything that would happen in John's life from that day forward, and that included all things inspiring and reprehensible. Woping Joe thought he was simply repaying a debt. John had helped him in the bar that night, so Woping Joe was obliged to return the favor. That is the Chinese way, and John would come to believe that it was the best part of a Chinese culture that has its roots going back thousands of years. Strength and loyalty to his brothers meant so much to John that he had the phrase tattooed on his arm. It was an indelible reminder of how to live.

"I'm never going to walk away from the people. They took care of me in my life. That's kind of a vow that you make; you never, ever walk away from the people that took care of you and care about you, 'cause that makes you no different from anybody else. Always honor your people. Honor your friends, your family. You know, respect and loyalty to your brothers that haven't ratted on you, you know what I mean? I'm not gonna change, not in that aspect."

John slept on the floor that night, but this time there was a carpet beneath him and the house, like his heart, was warm. John had found peace, and he found a family. The next day he would find another family, one even more long-lasting, one with dozens of fiercely loyal brothers willing to fight and die—or kill—for each other.

WOPING JOE brought John to a Vietnamese restaurant in Boston's Chinatown. This time, there were about twenty Asian gangsters demanding to know who John was and why he was there. Woping Joe vouched for John. They shared a meal of pork chops and rice with fish sauce, and John was in the gang. It was that easy. The rest of the initiation process included a shopping spree.

"I tried to say 'no,' but Woping Joe wasn't hearing that," John says. "So we went shopping and that was the beginning of my new life. It was the first time I ever went shopping without worrying about the price. If I didn't have enough to cover something, my new friends paid. I soon learned we all stood together as a family, and that was a feeling I'd been searching for my whole life."

As a white kid, John's assimilation into the Chinese gang culture was unprecedented, but surprisingly easy. He walked comfortably among a group of hard-core criminals, undaunted by the language barrier and the cultural differences, and free of any moral ambiguities that might have shown weakness or caused him to hesitate. He didn't judge them except to respect them, and that's what they were looking for in a recruit.

Each morning, there was a meeting at a restaurant called Dong Kahn, where several leaders of a local Asian gang comprised of Chinese and Vietnamese men discussed their gambling and drug business. The gambling was done inside Chinatown. The drugs were sold outside Chinatown. John was quickly passed off to another young Chinese man they called Eric. John lived with Eric and adopted the role of enforcer when it came time to collect gambling debts or drug money. John went from being a poor white kid to being a Chinese gangster literally overnight. It was an odd transformation, but one John adapted to very quickly. He loved learning about the Chinese culture, but he was actually being exposed to a mutated philosophy that exists only in the Asian underworld. While his gang leaders talked about and demanded respect, they routinely intimidated, extorted, and stole under a flag of self-righteousness that inexplicably satisfied a warped rationale for their violence and criminality.

"You might say, 'Normal people don't kill people,'" John begins. "Well, we were not normal people. Normal people don't deal with the things we deal with. We dealt with the street, but we dealt with it in a way that was, in our eyes, correct, you know? And that's just the way it goes."

It was all starting to make sense to John. A series of events and self-realizations answered the questions he had asked when he was cold and alone. When he faced danger or imposed pain on another human being without fear of consequences or reciprocity, and without so much as his pulse rising, he knew he was born for this. The extreme violence he was exposed to never shocked him or triggered a flight response. Rather, he found it suited his personality.

"I remember walking into a strip club in Chinatown, and I got jumped by some Italian gangsters," John recalls. "It was over a stripper who didn't make a difference to me. I didn't even know her real name. Well, some guy sucker punched me in the face. Broke my nose. And then another guy pulled out a big knife and went to stab me. As he pulls the knife out, the other guys grabbed me. So the kid I was with pulls out a Mac-10 machine gun. Thank God!"

John was seventeen years old when that happened. No shots were fired, but the appearance of the machine gun served as a warning. John casually walked to the bar with his friend, got some ice for his nose, ordered a drink, and stayed to watch the stripper who was at the heart of the altercation. Overall, it was a pretty good night.

After joining the gang, John spent about a year and a half in Boston's Chinatown working as muscle. His job was to be the imposing figure that stood by quietly while the Chinese and Vietnamese gang kids collected money from the gambling dens for their bosses. John's impact was significant, and it was rewarded with an opportunity to rise through the ranks. As if he were a legitimate businessman, he was transferred to New York, where he would receive additional training.

In order to reach his new home, John and a couple of Vietnamese gang kids stole two cars and drove to New York's Chinatown. As they parked along Canal Street and observed the mingling of merchants, customers, and tourists, the three teenage boys had no way of knowing they were in the middle of a war zone.

The opposing gang factions typically operated peacefully within their own zones of power and influence. The borders were well defined. Certain streets belonged to certain gangs. But well-established gangs like the Flying Dragons and Ghost Shadows were being threatened by extremely violent upstart gangs like the Green Dragons, and especially the Canal Boys, who preferred to be called Born To Kill, or BTK.

John was seventeen when he arrived in New York in 1988. By then, the Green Dragons were well on their way to taking over Queens, and a Vietnamese emigrant known as David Thai had broken away from the Flying Dragons and organized BTK. He gathered nearly one hundred Vietnamese refugees, spiked their hair, and dressed them in black suits with dark sunglasses. Together they terrorized merchants and shopkeepers throughout Brooklyn, the Bronx, and Queens with a rash of robberies, extortion, and extreme violence.

BTK solidified its reputation for using extreme measures in 1988 when its members threw a bomb into a police cruiser, injuring two officers. It was Thai's way of letting police know that he didn't appreciate several merchants under his control being arrested for selling fake Rolex watches. The brazen attack also served notice to police that BTK was at the forefront of Chinatown's growing phenomenon and incipient problem. There was an influx of unpredictable and uncontrollable Vietnamese gangs. And John moved right into the middle of it. Canal Street was the central place of operation for BTK, and John's first New York apartment was above a gambling den at 74 Canal Street.

This was the BTK's territory, but Thai was wise enough to work with instead of against the Hip Sing Association, one of the most powerful tongs in Chinatown. The tongs were secret brotherhoods and, like gangs, were powerful and often involved in criminal activity. Hip Sing was run by Benny Ong, known to law enforcement as the godfather of Chinatown, but known to everyone else as Uncle Seven, a nickname he received because he was the seventh child in his family. Uncle Seven had served seventeen years in prison for murder. He was convicted in 1937, when he was thirty years old, but whispers throughout Chinatown perpetuated a belief that Uncle Seven never committed the murder, but instead had taken the rap for someone more important within the organization. That kind of loyalty made him a hero in Chinatown, and a hero to John. David Thai decided it was wiser to make friends with an eighty-one-year-old legend than to go to war with him.

"Those Canal Boys, BTK, were friends with my boss," John says, referring to Uncle Seven. "Those guys ran around the country just killing and doing whatever they wanted to."

That, of course, created a number of enemies for BTK, and that led to the murder of Vinh Vu, an underboss in the gang and one of its most popular members. Vu's high profile made him an attractive target. So, on July 25, 1990, when Vu exited a massage parlor on Canal Street he was gunned down by several gunmen firing from the front- and backseat of a car. Three days later, Vu's funeral was disrupted at the cemetery when three gunmen opened fire on the mourners. Seven people were wounded.

"I was around when all this stuff happened," John says. "These guys were like my people, but these guys were renegades. They were crazy. They didn't follow the rules of the Chinese, because the majority of them were Vietnamese. When I grew up, there was a sense of loyalty to everybody. Like, we didn't just go out and cause problems. If you had an issue you had to talk to your boss to see what you could do. You didn't want to overstep your boundaries. There was honor. There was a sense of family."

Surrounded by the violence but not an active participant in the war, John went about the business of learning his trade. He watched how Uncle Seven conducted his business with a comforting presence and a firm hand. Although he walked with a cane, Uncle Seven seemed to glide through Chinatown with a dignified grace that accurately reflected his stature, but also belied his potential for cruelty. John thought about the time Uncle Seven served in prison for a murder he didn't commit, and he was inspired by the amount of respect Uncle Seven must have had for the real murderer. It saddened John to see that kind of respect disregarded by the next generation.

"I sit here in prison today," John says. "I could've told on people for murders and different things. But I'd rather take it and have my face, you know what I mean? People who put me in this position, the ones who ratted me out, there's always a time where people will have to pay the piper, one way or the other."

For gamblers who failed to pay, extorted merchants who complained, and robbery victims who dared to resist, the penalties were dramatic displays of force. John, who only needed a menacing glare or his fists to get people to hand over their money, was shocked the first time he and a few other gang members cased a check-cashing store. The men who delivered the cash to these stores were easy to spot. They were the ones with briefcases handcuffed to their wrists. When one man refused to give up his suitcase, someone in John's crew chopped off the man's hand with a machete. John watched the hand hit the ground, and then picked up the briefcase and ran. Later, he counted $40,000, and handed it over to a very pleased Uncle Seven.

"Yeah, I've seen guys get their hands chopped off," John says flatly. "This guy, first of all, he's involved in something he shouldn't have been involved in. I said, maybe my hand will be chopped next. Maybe I should learn a lesson from that."

On another occasion, John unknowingly went after a check-cashing business owned and operated by the Italian mafia. John got the money, but he was nearly killed in the attempt. While running down the street, John turned a corner and heard a loud shotgun blast. He looked back and saw a large hole in the wall next to him. That was his last check-cashing heist.

The first shots John ever fired from a gun were moments after he and his crew robbed an illegal sweatshop. He raced down the street with bullets whistling over his head, and while ducking and still running away, he reached back and fired wildly in the general direction of the shooters. Innocent bystanders could have been killed, but John was in survival mode.

"That really opened my eyes," John says. "This was for real. That was the first real sense I got that if I didn't shoot, I'd be dead."

Wanting desperately to impress Uncle Seven, John did as he was told and a little more. For instance, he learned to speak Chinese. John practiced constantly with his best friend in the group, a young Asian man who went by Sam.

"You have to speak Chinese," Sam told him. "How else will you get the girls?"

Sam began by teaching John one word at a time. Glass is "*boi*." Table is "*toi*." Door is "*munh*." John wrote them all down on flash cards, unconcerned with proper spelling. He just needed to pronounce the words correctly. Listening to a lot of Chinese music and singing songs at karaoke clubs helped. Watching dozens of Chinese movies with subtitles helped more. His favorite movie was *Moment of Romance*, starring Andy Lau as a gangster who falls in love with a good girl. John still relates to it well.

"I have the soundtrack, and I listen to it," he says. "It takes me back to when I was younger."

In the beginning, John often spoke in broken Chinese, and he routinely spoke it backward, but he was happy to be understood and proud to be respected.

"It wasn't me that taught myself Chinese," John says humbly. "God taught me. He gave me what I needed to survive."

John's fluency in the language didn't happen until he began living with the Laus, a Chinese couple, in Queens. They taught him to speak fluent Chinese with an authentic *Toi Son* accent, and they instilled in John the importance of Buddhism as part of his new Chinese culture. John soaked it all in, and he had no trouble reconciling the life lessons he learned and the actual life he was leading.

"Before I did anything, I prayed," John says.

While he was living with Jackie Lau, who, along with his brother Peter Lau, owned businesses in Manhattan's Chinatown and Queens, John settled into place as an enforcer and a bodyguard. It was another opportunity for him to see firsthand how Chinese leaders ran their operations. The very fact that he was living with his boss told him that in this insular world people took care of their own. And John, in turn, would take care of them.

As their armed bodyguard, John traveled with Jackie and Peter all over the country as they tended to a variety of business interests. John enjoyed visiting new cities, but he especially loved the fast-paced energy of New York. Being with the Lau brothers gave John a special status and certain privileges. He was with them when they frequented an underground club at the Hollywood Bowl on Woodhaven Boulevard where high-priced escorts flirted in sexy outfits.

The first time John went to the club, he entered nervously. He was concerned that the off-duty police officers guarding the door would take his gun from him when the alarm went off on the metal detectors, but the cops just waved him through. Once inside, John still had a job to do, so he didn't drink or pick up women, but he beamed with pride as he looked around and realized that he had made it. He fit in at a place filled with rich and powerful people. He was a little over two years removed from starving on his kitchen floor, and now he had more money than he knew what to do with. John's primary job was to collect protection money from neighborhood stores, but he made most of his money robbing the gambling dens. He and his crew even robbed the cooks at restaurants on payday for what little money those men had. John also got involved with running drugs, and eventually, selling them himself.

He also learned the fine art of a specific form of extortion known as *Wat Yan*. It was a simple process of letting rich Asian college students or foreign businessmen get drunk enough to start shooting their mouths off. Once they realized they had insulted the wrong people, they paid whatever it took to escape the consequences.

One night when a few of the other men who lived at Jackie's house in Queens got into a fight, a New York City SWAT team showed up and stormed the house with guns drawn. Shots were fired and one of Jackie's men was killed.

Jackie was arrested along with his brother Peter who had pulled a gun on the cops and threatened them. One of the very few Asian police officers on the force was able to calm everyone down and avoid further bloodshed. John was not arrested, so it was his responsibility to collect the funds necessary to bail out everyone else. It was part of the code.

"We follow a set of rules," John explains. "If you're my brother, that means something. You stick together. God forbid, you get arrested and your bail is twenty thousand dollars. Well, we're all running around with big, thick, gold bracelets on that are worth eight to ten thousand bucks. You take them off. You trade them in to get the money, and you get your brother out. No thoughts. No nothing. You do it."

But rules come with consequences, and in John's Chinese family, the consequences were often severe. One of John's gang brothers named Tony had escalated the fight at the house that resulted in the SWAT team raid. Tony wasn't killed for his unintended mistake, but he did have his legs broken. John brought Tony to Chinatown where two other men enforced the order. Tony understood.

John also understood that gang violence and retaliation were simply the result of those gangs playing by the rules. So, when a disc jockey working at Jackie and Peter's waterfront nightclub was shot in the head and killed in October of 1990, John understood it was a proper response to the BTK shooting at the funeral three months earlier. After all, the DJ was a member of Ghost Shadows. And John wasn't surprised when one week after the DJ's murder, three members of BTK were killed execution style right out in front of the Lau's club.

After his nearly two years of residency-like training was completed in New York, John moved back to Boston's Chinatown. He quickly learned that the FBI was watching him closely. It was the early fall of 1990, and John was walking down Beach Street in Chinatown when he noticed a dark car driving slowly by him. When the car went by for the third time, John jumped in front of the car, forcing it to stop. John slammed both his palms down onto the hood. The passenger in the front seat of the vehicle rolled down his window and called out to John.

"Uncle Seven's dead!"

The man spoke unemotionally and John, despite learning someone he greatly respected had died, reacted the same way. He walked over to the passenger side of the car where the man identified himself as an FBI agent and showed John his badge.

"Why you telling me?" John asked. "I don't know anybody named Uncle Seven."

"No?" the agent asked, surprised. "Ever been to New York?"

"Nope. Just a Dorchester kid. Never been nowhere."

At that point, the agent pulled out a surveillance photo of John in New York wearing the exact jacket he was wearing now.

"Wanna change your answer?" the agent asked.

"You wanna go fuck yourself?" John replied.

With that as his exit line, John put both hands on the roof of the car and did a short drumbeat. He walked away with his head held high and his chest puffed out. He thought about his clever response to the agent, and he smiled. He realized he was important enough to be harassed by the FBI, and his smile grew. Yes, it was another good day in Chinatown.

TWO

THE ROOM WAS DARK, and the young Asian men in it were unnerved by the mystery created by the blackness, the smell of incense, the sharp knives, and the distinctive sound of a live chicken. Red wine was poured into a porcelain bowl and placed in the middle of a tall round table. Each man was told to cut his own finger with a knife until several droplets of blood dripped into the bowl. As the men followed the order, someone raised a small hatchet in the darkness, and swung down with enough fury and force to successfully behead the chicken. The body of the bird was tipped upside down until much of its blood spilled into the bowl, and the men were given one final order. Those who showed any reluctance had a cleaver pressed against the back of their heads. That was enough motivation to convince each man to do as commanded. They drank the mixture of human and chicken blood. Thus, the initiation ceremony was complete, and they were all new members of the Ping On gang in Boston's Chinatown.

This had long been the initiation ceremony for all new members. In 1990, however, when John returned from New York and pledged his allegiance to Ping On, blood rituals like this were no longer typical. John needed only to be sponsored, and Peter Lau took care of that. Lau flew up from New York and vouched for John to a man named Bai Ming, and that was good enough for entry into the gang. Bai Ming had recently become next in line to take over Ping On, which would make him the most powerful man in Boston's Chinatown, but to assume control, two things had to happen. First, the current leader would have to abdicate the throne, and a bloody war had to be won. When it was over, only one man would be standing, and John Willis, the loyal soldier, would be standing right next to him. The last leader of Ping On was Bai Ming. The first was Stephen Tse. In between, there were several who were killed while wearing the crown.

Stephen Tse, also known as Sky Dragon, was the godfather of Chinatown. He came to the United States from Hong Kong in the early 1970s, settling first in New York before moving to Boston. After serving a short sentence for a home invasion in Brookline, Massachusetts, he was released from jail in 1977, and immediately joined the Hung Mun tong, which presented itself as a social club but was really a base of operation for organized crime in Chinatown. Sky Dragon began recruiting lieutenants to carry out his extortion orders and run his gambling dens, which eventually led to the formation of Ping On. His rise to power was swift, in part because in 1979 Boston's Ghost Shadows were needed in New York to participate in an ongoing gang war. When the Ghost Shadows took their eye off the ball in Boston, Sky Dragon seized control.

Sky Dragon built his criminal empire by modeling Ping On after centuries-old triads, or underground criminal societies that had their roots in China. Sky Dragon was a ranking member of the 14K triad in Hong Kong, and his reputation was solidified in 1983 when he was one of several triad kingpins who met in Hong Kong and agreed to an international brotherhood of cooperation. Peter Chin, head of the Ghost Shadows in New York, and Danny Mo, leader of the Kung Lok triad in Toronto, were also at the summit. They burned yellow paper to indicate the start of a new venture, and together they began an extremely lucrative heroin trafficking business.

Sky Dragon was able to rise to power primarily through intimidation and threats of violence. The dozens of young men he recruited and united were enough to demonstrate a show of force throughout Chinatown that left businessmen, pimps, and prostitutes very little choice. The power of Ping On was in the numbers, and as a result, Sky Dragon's extortion of legal and illegal businesses required mostly threats and very little violence. With an army on his side, Sky Dragon could walk into any business or approach any individual and ask: "What's it worth to you to refuse me?"

Businessmen were quick to understand the logic behind the system. Extortion became an overhead expense, and protection money was an investment in a security system. Businessmen who paid had nothing to worry about. Those who refused would be taking the risk that seventy gang kids might bust up their shops and restaurants, or they might ruin businesses by simply hanging out in front of them, thereby scaring away customers. Pimps and illegal gamblers couldn't stand up to seventy gang kids either, and no one was willing to solicit the help of the police.

"In Chinese culture," John explains, "it's been happening for a thousand years. Organizations protect and take care of their people. Well, in Chinatown, we did the same thing. We protected, took care of the people. And the people know who they are. When they needed money to open a business, they came to the gangsters. They didn't go to the bank. When they needed to, you know, put in a new addition on their house, they came to the gangsters. When they wanted to build a bigger restaurant, you know, out in the suburbs, they came to the gangsters. And that's fine. And everybody paid their money. It may be something we would perceive as really screwed up, like extortion and different shit amongst businesses, like it's all these people preying on the weak, but that isn't the way it was."

Sky Dragon ran Boston's Chinatown in relative anonymity for several years. He appeared to local law enforcement as a law-abiding citizen who simply managed the Kung Fu restaurant on Tyler Street. Even the members of his gang tended to hold one or more low-paying jobs, which was not a common trait among criminals outside of Chinatown.

It was an intentional effort on Sky Dragon's part to hide his gang activity from the police. It worked quite well until a witness testified before President Ronald Reagan's Commission on Organized Crime in 1984 that Sky Dragon was the head of Ping On, which the witness described as a "hard-core" gang with nearly one hundred members. The witness identified himself as a former member of the Ghost Shadows. Fearing for his life, the witness gave his testimony from behind a wooden screen, and kept his face buried beneath a hood, and only agreed to speak if his voice were altered.

The witness told the commission that Ping On was involved in everything from racketeering and prostitution to gambling and loansharking. The commission responded by calling Sky Dragon in to testify. He refused. He explained that Ping On's "ritualistic vows of secrecy" forbade him from speaking, and he invoked his Fifth Amendment right eighty times. Of course, in acknowledging the vows of secrecy, he effectively admitted his role in the gang.

Sky Dragon wasn't just loyal to an oath, however. He also told a judge that the tendency of the gang to "resort to violence against those violating such vows" made it unwise for him to testify. Sky Dragon may have been concerned about a small Asian man who burst into his Kung Fu restaurant wielding a gun and threatening to wipe out the place, or he may have believed the Boston police detective who told him there was a $10,000 bounty on his head. Either way, Sky

Dragon wasn't talking. Even the leader of the gang was afraid of reprisal from the gang.

Sky Dragon was offered immunity and given the chance to join the Witness Protection Program, but he told the commission he would rather go to prison, and so he did. Sky Dragon was held in civil contempt and sent to the Essex County House of Correction in Lawrence, Massachusetts. Sky Dragon served sixteen months of a maximum eighteen-month sentence.

While he was away, his criminal enterprise suffered and an influx of new gangs infiltrated Ping On territory. The Ghost Shadows moved back into Boston. Immediately upon Sky Dragon's release from prison, they put out an order to have him assassinated. Local police inadvertently foiled the plot when they noticed a suspicious car with New York plates driving along Beach Street in Chinatown. They stopped the car and discovered three members of Ghost Shadows carrying an arsenal of automatic weapons.

When he was released from prison, Sky Dragon found himself in the middle of a very different Chinatown. The new Vietnamese gangs were far more willing to use violence first and make threats later. Sky Dragon was forced to step up his game.

He began by taking a ruthless killer under his wing. That man was a young Vietnamese criminal named Ay-yat, who coincidentally had grown up in Vietnam as Bai Ming's neighbor. Sky Dragon met Ay-yat in prison, learned of his connection to Bai Ming, and recruited him to join Ping On when he got out of jail. Ay-yat knew of Sky Dragon's reputation and was honored by the invitation. Ay-yat became a loyal follower and made it his life's mission to impress Sky Dragon in any way he could, and that included luring a man to his death.

Sky Dragon got out of prison in March of 1986. Ay-yat was released a few months later, and within a year, a high-rolling gambler who had befriended and then betrayed Sky Dragon was dead.

Son Van Vu was a frequent player at Sky Dragon's gambling dens and had no problem betting $5,000 a hand. He also had no problem robbing the same gambling dens with his Vietnamese gang cohorts. Unbeknownst to Sky Dragon at the time, Vu was part of a gang that defied Ping On's control over Chinatown. They extorted money and robbed businesses known to be in Ping On territory.

At the time, Sky Dragon and Vu were friends, even travel companions. They took several trips to New York and California together to gamble and conduct drug deals. Sky Dragon was trafficking heroin and cocaine, and Vu was becoming a coke addict. Their friendship ended when Sky Dragon discovered Vu was involved in a robbery at one of his gambling dens. It's possible Ay-yat was the one to inform Sky Dragon, because he had also become a close friend and confidant of Vu's. Sky Dragon decided to use that friendship to his advantage and he paid Ay-yat $30,000 to kill Vu.

The plan was simple. The next time Vu traveled to California, Ay-yat would follow him out and kill him there. Sky Dragon explained that investigators would be less likely to look for suspects three thousand miles away. Ay-yat understood and was excited to have the opportunity to show Sky Dragon his courage and loyalty. There was nothing he wouldn't do for Sky Dragon, and without hesitation, he carried out the order to kill Vu on December 9, 1986, in Hollywood, California. Sky Dragon was in Hong Kong at the time.

Vu had a home in Oakland, California, and regularly went across the country to visit a couple of his favorite gambling dens in the Bay Area. He flew out in late October and welcomed his friend Ay-yat about a month later. He showed off his brand-new gray BMW 325E he had just purchased with his gambling proceeds, and the two friends shared many laughs. Vu was on a hot streak and feeling good, but his coke habit had gotten worse, which may explain why his already slight 5-foot-5 frame was thirty pounds lighter when Ay-yat saw him again. Not that it would matter. Vu would only be alive for a few more days.

It appears Ay-yat convinced Vu to take a ride with him. Where they were going is unclear, but they traveled four hundred miles before checking into the Hollywood Premier Motel at 5:10 in the morning. Ay-yat waited in the car while Vu checked in at the front desk. Later, as Vu slept, Ay-yat put a gun to his head and shot him once behind each ear. Later that day, when a chambermaid knocked and entered the room, she saw Vu lying facedown and shirtless. On his bare back was a large tattoo of the Statue of Liberty. Vu had gotten the tattoo soon after arriving in America.

"This was a straight professional hit," Detective Butch Harris of the Hollywood homicide bureau told the *Boston Globe*. "They left the gun behind, but nothing else. In a case like this, it's not uncommon to send a good friend in to arrange (the murder) or carry it out."

Vu's wife alerted police that Ay-yat had gone out to California to visit her husband. Ay-yat was interviewed about the murder and was considered a prime suspect, but investigators didn't have enough evidence. The case wouldn't be solved for another twelve years, when Ay-yat finally admitted to committing the execution-style killing at the request of his Ping On boss, Sky Dragon.

The murder seemed to embolden Ay-yat, and less than a month later, he was arrested following a jewelry store robbery in Lowell, Massachusetts. Police called it one of the most violent robberies the area had ever seen, and they were able to watch it on the store's surveillance video. What they saw was a sixteen-year-old male walk into the store and jump onto the back of the store's owner, Nguon Bunn Tea. While Tea wrestled with the teenager, seven other hoodlums entered the store and began smashing hammers on top of the jewelry cases. But the cases didn't break!

Tea had been victimized twice before when his store was located in Boston's Chinatown. As recently as October, gang members made off with about $110,000 in jewelry. Scared and frustrated, Tea had moved away and relocated in Lowell. When the gang discovered where he'd gone, they vindictively targeted him again. However, they had no way of knowing that instead of glass cases, Tea would equip this store with a new unbreakable plastic. As the hammers bounced off the counters, the gang grew frustrated, and one of the members smashed Tea's wife, Mon Ly, with his gun instead. She suffered a fractured skull, but survived. The eight assailants took off without any loot. Police captured them a short distance away.

The robbery had not been sanctioned by Sky Dragon, and he was not happy that Ay-yat was freelancing with his own criminal enterprise, or that innocent people were getting hurt, which meant the heat from police would intensify. Sky Dragon had run a mostly bloodless regime in Chinatown, in part because he knew he could get away with it. He hated his time in jail and had vowed never to go back. Now, he had a loose cannon working for him, and it made him nervous. So, he cut ties with Ay-yat. It was meant to be a punishment and a warning to others, but Ay-yat saw it as an opportunity. He formed his own gang, known as the Ah Sing Boys, and continued his string of robberies, home invasions, and murders. During his reign of terror, he would frequently cross paths with John Willis.

"As far as Ay-yat," John Willis says, "he is a good brother of mine. He is like an older brother to me, and yes, he is a very dangerous man!"

SKY DRAGON was arrested again in January of 1989, for gambling, of all things.

Sky Dragon was playing the popular Asian games of chance, pai gow and mahjongg, inside the gambling den at 32 Oxford Street. It was the den for high rollers, and twenty-three of them were arrested when police burst in and broke up the games. There was $21,506 in cash on the table where Sky Dragon was playing. It was a rare bust of routine gambling. Police could break into nearly two dozen such dens on any night of the week, but they seldom bothered. Gambling was part of the culture. There was little effort to hide it, and the community never asked for the anti-gaming laws to be enforced.

"This isn't who we're looking for," then–Police Superintendent Joseph Saja said. "We try to concentrate on the gambling where organized crime is involved."

Sky Dragon spent the night in jail, but was freed on bail at his arraignment the next day. It's unlikely Sky Dragon would have received jail time for an infraction as insignificant as gambling, but he felt like the heat was on, and he wasn't willing to take any chances. So, he paid his $50 fine and left immediately for Hong Kong, where he spent the better part of the next two years running a bean sprout business. It was a sincere effort to return to legitimacy, and it might have rung the death knell for Ping On.

Instead, infighting and the struggle for power went on for years, until finally one man would stand on top: Bai Ming, aided by John Willis.

THREE

A SLENDER IRISHMAN with cheeks reddened by the cold and eyes watering from the wind rapidly shoveled snow from the sidewalk along Tyler Street in Boston's Chinatown. Neither his green jacket nor his thin gloves were qualified to adequately protect him from the latest winter snowstorm. The only sounds he heard were his own heavy breathing and the rhythmic scraping of his shovel against the cement. Three inches of snow had already fallen and three more were still to come. The Irishman looked up through the flurries and watched a blue Toyota sedan drive slowly by him. It was notable because of the dark-tinted windows, and because it was the first car he'd seen in over two hours. The Irishman checked his watch and noted it was just after 4:00 A.M.

He blew once into his cupped hands in a feeble effort to warm them up, and returned to work. The blue Toyota circled the block and made another pass down Tyler Street. This time the car drove even more slowly. The Irishman couldn't see who was in the car, but he was certain someone inside it was watching him. Uneasily, he ducked his head, turned up his collar, and began shoveling even more rapidly. His wish that the Toyota would vanish came true.

Some fifteen minutes later the Irishman had reached the doorway of a Chinese-Vietnamese after-hours social club at 85A Tyler Street. Just then two police cars pulled up. Their blue lights were flashing, but the sirens were off. The policemen jumped out of the cars with guns drawn and swung open the door to the social club. The Irishman peered inside and saw five bodies slumped over with their heads lying flat on a table. More police arrived and each time the door swung open, the Irishman saw a little more clearly. There were playing cards and money on the table, and the men were covered in blood. The Irishman heard the shouts from the policemen and the call for an ambulance. And what he learned is that he had stumbled upon what would forever be identified as the Tyler Street Massacre. He took a few steps backward before turning on his heels and hastening away. He shivered as he walked, but not so much from the cold as from the thought of his narrow escape. Did the blue Toyota with the dark-tinted windows hide the face of a killer? And if the windows hadn't been tinted, thus allowing the Irishman to see inside, would he have been victim number six that night?

JOHN WILLIS had had breakfast with victim number one the morning before the Tyler Street Massacre. On January 11, 1991, he sat in a corner booth at Dong Khanh on Harrison Avenue and enjoyed a bowl of pho, a Vietnamese rice noodle soup served with a rare steak cooked in hot water. Across the table sat his good friend and breakfast companion, Dai Keung, a man whom Sky Dragon had attempted to kill a few years earlier simply because Dai Keung wanted to receive payment of a $30,000 debt from Sky Dragon in Sky Dragon's own Kung Fu restaurant, which was an obvious and intentional show of disrespect.

"Have I died?" Sky Dragon bellowed.

Sky Dragon was equally upset with a former Ping On member named Chao Va Meng, who also asked to receive a payoff inside the Kung Fu restaurant. Sky Dragon ordered two hit men to kill Dai Keung and Chao Va Meng, demanding that they "shoot them in the testicles until they burst." The assassins failed in their attempt despite firing thirty shots at Keung and Meng as they walked through a Tyler Street parking lot. John was aware of the tension between Sky Dragon and Dai Keung, but Sky Dragon was hiding out in

Hong Kong, and Dai Keung was an amiable gangster who frequently flew to and from San Francisco. When he was in town, he usually found time for John.

"He treated me like a brother," John says. "We hung out in gambling places. He was a pretty crazy guy. He ran around with another guy named Peter. They fought with machine guns in California. California was more aggressive. A lot of fighting."

Unbeknownst to John, that aggression was becoming bicoastal. Dai Keung's gang boss in San Francisco, Peter Chong, was making plans to take over Asian organized crime from Boston and New York to San Francisco and everywhere in between. His intention was to form an umbrella organization called Tien Ha Wui, or "Whole Earth Society." If successful, the Whole Earth Society would put Sky Dragon, or those vying to replace him in his absence, out of business. It appears Chong sent Dai Keung to Boston to establish a foothold there. It also appears that Dai Keung was the first killed, and the primary target of the Tyler Street Massacre. Furthermore, Hun Suk, Sky Dragon's most trusted lieutenant, is alleged to have been one of the shooters.

It's quite possible Dai Keung was attempting to get close to John, because John had established himself as Bai Ming's right-hand man immediately upon his return from New York. John's rapid ascendance in the gang occurred when he exhibited fierce loyalty to his brothers. Despite knowing the FBI had him under surveillance, John reacted the only way he knew how when he discovered Woping Joe's brother Nathan had been badly beaten by a rival gang. Nathan's eye had been knocked out of its socket and he was laid up in the hospital. No retaliatory measures were planned, and John couldn't stand for it.

"We've got to do something about this," John shouted at Woping Joe and his crew. "Let's go!"

John grabbed a Mac-10 machine gun and led the gang down to the building where the presumed assailants lived. John spotted the guys they were after and shot at them several times. It was a bold move of leadership and Bai Ming took notice. From that moment on, John spent nearly every day at Ming's side. Ming became his mentor, and John became Ming's enforcer and protector.

"There were loyal things he did, like you know, I always had the best clothes, the best sneakers. He'd take me shopping. Different guys, he'd pay for their medical bills and different things. He was definitely the brother that you needed to have when you were young."

Now, as Dai Keung schemed with Peter Chong to take over the Boston gangs, it's reasonable to think Dai Keung was making friends with John and earning his trust in order to get close to Ming. It's a theory Ming himself may have considered.

After breakfast, John and Dai Keung made plans to get together later that night. First, however, John was charged with driving Woping Joe's older brother, Wah Ming, to the airport.

"Me and another kid named Manny dropped him off at the airport," John recalls. "Manny (which isn't his real name) used to sell a lot of drugs, cocaine mostly. It was probably about ten thirty at night when he got a call to bring some coke to Chinatown for Dai Keung. We were at Boston Billiards at the time, and when we went outside it was snowing. We still had Wah Ming's new Mercedes, which we weren't supposed to be driving. We were supposed to take it back to his house. The streets of Chinatown are very thin and congested. So, I said, 'I'm not going over there with this car. We're gonna get in trouble,' but we ended up going anyway."

Cautiously, John drove the Mercedes through the snow out of the Fenway neighborhood and down Brookline Avenue. Still a few miles from Chinatown, John hit a massive snow-covered pothole. That thud was followed by the distinctive thumping sound a flat tire makes. The car swerved toward a line of parked cars, but John was able to get it under control without hitting anything.

"Fuck it! Let's leave," John said to Manny as they changed the right front tire. "Let's go back!"

John was rather convincing standing there with a lug wrench in his hands, and Manny agreed to turn back around. John got back to his apartment in Forest Hills about one in the morning, and he received a call less than four hours later.

"Don't come to Chinatown," the voice on the other end commanded. John recognized the voice, and was prepared to obey the directive.

"Okay," he said, "but why not?"

"Just don't come. You'll find out soon enough. Tell everybody to stay home!"

John awoke the next morning to the news that five men had been killed, his friend Dai Keung among them. Word spread quickly through the streets, but even street rumors, often the most reliable source, were merely conjecture.

"They came to get Dai Keung," John says with conviction. "They shot them all, but Dai Keung is who they wanted. I don't know exactly why he was killed. It was probably some kind of power struggle. People might have felt like he was going to cause problems. It was said through the Chinese community that Hun Suk's people did it."

John's account is corroborated by the two men who survived the massacre: Pak Wing Lee and Billy Yu Man Young. Lee miraculously survived a gunshot to the head. Young, unfavorably nicknamed "Wrinkled Skin Man," was the owner of the club and was spared by the killers. Years after the shooting, both men would testify to what happened.

"Robbery!" three men shouted as they burst into the club. "Don't move!"

But this was clearly not a robbery. When police arrived, there were several hundred dollars strewn on top of the card table. The money was splattered with blood and brains from the gunshot wounds to the victims' heads.

Lee claimed that Hun Suk shouted the orders and told each man in the club to lie facedown on the floor. Hun Suk then strode purposefully over to Dai Keung and put a gun to the back of his head.

"Please, don't shoot! I'm begging you!"

Those were Dai Keung's last words before Hun Suk put two bullets in the back of his head.

Lee heard more pleading followed by more gunshots.

"I'll be a horse. I'll be a dog," one man cried. "I'll be anything. Don't shoot."

Lee didn't move except when the gunshots startled him. He thought about fate's role in all of this and regretted his decision to brave the snowstorm and come to the club that night. He was a cook at an Ipswich restaurant and had been to this gambling den many times before. Most recently, he had lost a bit of money and had returned to square his debt with the "Wrinkled Skin Man." He remembers feeling the barrel of Hun Suk's gun on the back of his head.

"Don't fire the gun! Don't!" Lee begged. He would later testify: "He did not listen to me. He fired. Then I did not know anything."

Lee lay unconscious for thirty minutes, but he survived the shooting when the bullet broke into fragments and merely fractured his skull, but did not penetrate his brain. When he eventually regained consciousness, the shooters were gone. He crawled to the back door of the club and called out for help. Someone from a nearby apartment called the police. Lee was taken to Massachusetts General Hospital, where he remained for several weeks before being released into the Witness Protection Program.

Moments after Lee was wounded, Hun Suk ordered one of the other shooters, Siny Van Tran, to "kill, kill, kill that Wrinkled Skin Man!"

Young began pleading for his life.

"If you want money, if you want gold, I'll give you all. Please don't shoot!"

Tran froze. He looked first at Hun Suk hoping he would change his mind, or redirect the order to the third shooter, Nam The Tham. But while those two men were busy shooting the other victims, Tran whispered urgently and gestured to Young to run away.

Tran maintains that he was only at the club to buy cocaine, and that he didn't shoot anyone. He claims he didn't even have a gun. Two guns were found at the scene. Neither had his fingerprints on them. He also denied Young's accusation that he spent most of the night going in and out of the club and was probably the one who notified the other shooters that he had found their target. Tham's account differs. He claims Tran and Hun Suk were the shooters.

"It was very cruel," Tham said in a police interview. "I saw them shoot. I couldn't even stand steady."

Tham also told investigators that not only was Dai Keung the intended target, but so too was Wrinkled Skin Man. That, of course, seems unlikely, considering Wrinkled Skin Man wasn't even shot. Within a week of the shooting, murder warrants were issued for the arrest of the three gunmen identified by Lee. The mayor of Boston, Raymond Flynn, who had gone to the scene in time to see the body bags being taken out of the club, said, "We have to chase the guys responsible for this, even if we have to go to the ends of the earth."

He may have been somewhat prescient, because they found the gunmen seven years later on the other side of the world. When Tham, Tran, and Hun Suk fled the scene, perhaps in the blue Toyota spotted by the Irishman, they drove straight to Atlantic City, where they gambled for days. Upon hearing that Lee had survived the shooting, Tham, Tran, and Hun Suk went to the Philadelphia International Airport and escaped to Hong Kong. There they stayed in the Chinese underworld until 1998, when Tran and Tham were arrested by the Chinese government for unrelated crimes, including drug possession. It took three more years to convince China to extradite them back to the United States.

The delicate negotiations looked to be falling apart until investigators caught a break in April of 2001. The FBI arrested one of China's most wanted fugitives, Qin Hong, in New York. Hong was wanted in China for millions of dollars' worth of fraud, a crime punishable by death. The United States deported him to Peru, which sent him back to China. Six months later, Tran and Tham were extradited back to Boston. They were arraigned on murder charges the day after Christmas 2001 in Suffolk Superior Court in Boston. In 2005, they were found guilty and sentenced to life in prison. Judge Stephen Neel emphasized the "particularly heinous" nature of the killings and ordered the five life sentences run consecutively without the possibility of parole. Tran laughed out loud as the sentence was read.

Among the credible theories to explain the motive behind the Tyler Street Massacre is that Sky Dragon reached out from Hong Kong and finally exacted his vengeance upon Dai Keung for the disrespect shown to him years earlier, and the others killed were collateral damage. The FBI certainly finds that plausible. Their intelligence indicates Sky Dragon fled to Hong Kong in January of 1989, but that he returned at least twice, once in May of that year, and again in October of 1990. Perhaps not coincidentally, his traveling companion for that second trip back to the United States was Hun Suk. Three months later, Hun Suk shot and killed Dai Keung.

Of further interest to investigators is that Hun Suk, Tran, and Tham all worked for Sky Dragon at one time or another. Now, Hun Suk may have been a loyal soldier under Sky Dragon, or he may have acted alone as he sought to exert power and control of Chinatown's gambling dens. It wasn't long after Sky Dragon had left Boston that Hun Suk put together a gang of nearly two hundred men who helped him control Chinatown's westernmost edge along lower Washington Street. Police believe he paid Sky Dragon tribute money for the right to sell drugs, run gambling dens, and control a small prostitution ring.

Hun Suk and another crime boss, named Wayne Kwong, were vying for sole power of Chinatown, and their fiercest rival was Bai Ming. These were the heads of the three most active and powerful gangs in Boston in the early 1990s. Hun Suk appears to have been Sky Dragon's choice to take over, but Hun Suk fled from authorities after the Tyler Street Massacre. So, with him out of the picture, only Wayne Kwong stood in Bai Ming's way of achieving exclusive power in Chinatown.

FOUR

I'VE BEEN TO a lot more funerals than birthday parties," John Willis often repeats with a smile.

Surrounded by death, yet so full of life, John suddenly found himself feeling weak and lethargic, and he was urinating a lot. Instead of going to a doctor, he decided it was time for the first vacation of his life. He went to Rock Hill, South Carolina, to visit his uncle.

"I was riding my uncle's horse, and people going by kept waving," John recalls fondly. "I went back and told my uncle, 'Hey, everybody knows your horse.' He said, 'That's just people saying hi.' I thought it was the greatest thing in the world."

And then he passed out. He doesn't know how long he was out, only that when he awoke, there were five doctors staring down at him.

"What's going on?" John asked groggily.

"We're trying to figure out why you're still alive," one of the doctors explained.

John was not quite twenty years old when he found out the hard way that he's a type 1 diabetic. When he was taken to the hospital in South Carolina, his blood sugar was 1,680 mg/dL. Non-diabetics tend to fluctuate between 70 and 140 mg/dL. John was supposed to be dead. Instead, he was released from the hospital five days later, and before heading back to Boston, he went to see his father on the nearby Catawba reservation.

"To be honest with you, I went to hurt him," John admits. "I didn't bring a knife or a gun. I didn't need anything. But I gave him a chance to talk, and he told me his reason for leaving me when I was a kid. He said my mother was not his true love."

John accepted the explanation and later repeated the behavior. He met a hostess at a Chinese restaurant named Joy, who looked like Sandra Bullock with blonde hair. She was a nice girl from a nice family, and John thought he was in love. They got married when John was twenty, and they had two sons just about a year apart. They even bought a house, but John was not ready to be domesticated. More loyal to his gang than to his young family, he was soon divorced, and he has no relationship at all with his sons.

John returned from South Carolina in late March of 1991 and heard the news that his friend Ay-yat had been charged with the murder of three men at the A Don restaurant on College Street in Toronto, Canada. It was apparently a spontaneous killing over a woman. The victims were strangers with whom Ay-yat had had an altercation at a nightclub. Ay-yat and two other men walked into the restaurant and opened fire. Additionally, by the end of the summer in 1991, ten members of Ay-yat's rival gang were assassinated, and word spread quickly on the streets of Boston that even though Ay-yat was in prison, he might have been ordering the hits.

"When he came back out," John says, "he was going to be part of us. We were getting stronger and stronger, but unfortunately he got into an argument with someone."

In September of 1991, John was staying with Chay Giang, a member of Ay-yat's Ah Singh Boys, in a house in Malden. Giang's family was very close to Bai Ming, and that gave Giang a special place in Ping On. So, John was looking out for Giang, and the two became very good friends. John listened as Giang talked enthusiastically about moving in with his girlfriend, Lynn, who had faithfully waited for him to get out of jail. He also listened as Giang spoke about the growing tension between himself and a tough Dorchester kid named Atoy. It got to a point where John thought it was time to settle the matter. His intention was to peaceably talk it out, and a meeting was arranged. The plan was to meet in the open in broad daylight, which would reduce the likelihood of any violence breaking out, but when John arrived at the Tyler Street parking lot, he noticed Atoy had a large bag over his shoulder. John immediately ordered his boys to get the guns they kept stashed in nearby locations, but the guns weren't where they were supposed to be.

"Somebody had moved our guns," John says. "We went into the gambling house and got some bats. By the time we got there, Giang and Atoy were arguing. We approached and Giang slapped Atoy real hard. Then Atoy shot through the bag. Three in the chest. Three in the head. His shit went everywhere."

As John stood there with a baseball bat over his shoulder, he was momentarily stunned. His good friend's blood and guts were all over him and they felt warm on his face and hands. He watched as Atoy turned and pointed the gun directly at him.

"I froze," John recalls. "And then he pulled the trigger."

But nothing happened. The gun jammed and Atoy ran away. John bent down and picked up the limp body of his friend.

"You could see the holes through his head," John says. "He was dead."

And at that moment, the skies opened up and a torrential rain flooded the parking lot. John, unable to do anything for Giang, and not wanting to be around when the police arrived, got up and left hurriedly. As he got to the entrance to the parking lot, a car was pulling in.

"Damn!" he thought. "It's Giang's mother."

He put up his hand to stop her from coming into the parking lot, and motioned to her to pull the car beside the sidewalk. John turned his back to Giang's mother for a moment and wiped away some of her son's blood. He was thankful the rain was helping to disguise it, and then he got into the car.

"Where's Giang?" she asked.

"Let's just get out of here," John said.

After she had driven a few blocks down the street, John told her what had happened. She sobbed as any mother would do, and John found himself helpless to console her.

"That was the first murder that mattered to me," John says. "There's a side of this that people don't understand. We live and enjoy life just like normal people. When we're extorting money, we're not being bullies like people think. That's part of the culture. These people came here and borrowed money to start a business, and they have to pay it back. The business community understands that, but that murder made me really understand why people feared us, because you could be standing there talking one minute and the next minute be dead."

Giang was taken to Boston City Hospital with gunshot wounds to his head and chest, and according to police reports, he died in the emergency room. Atoy was never arrested. It's believed he went back home to Vietnam, but when some of John's gang members were sent there to look for him, Atoy was nowhere to be found.

The murder of Chay Giang occurred in the same parking lot where John and his gang routinely ran reconnaissance. They used the same Motorola radios the police used, and they ran military-style protocols throughout sections of Chinatown. Each gang member was assigned a specific location where he would stand as sentry and communicate any suspicious activity, and they were particularly suspicious of strangers, anyone from out of town, and young Asian men who were unknown to them.

"It was a very complex system in Chinatown," John explains. "We checked everybody. If we didn't know you, we stopped you on the street. Patted you down. If you came from New York, we wanted to go through your car. We wanted to know who you were. There's a lot of stuff going on. There's a lot of people trying to come in and take over. There's a lot of fighting."

The extra precautions appear to have been warranted. In 1991 alone, there were nine homicides within the forty-six acres of Chinatown. John's due diligence avoided a tenth. He recalls the warm August night when he was at a karaoke bar around the corner from the old Boston Garden in North Station. Bai Ming and a few of his fellow gang members were there as well. When an argument occurred between their group and another, John knew it was time to get Ming out of there. John hustled Ming into a car, pounded on the roof, and the driver peeled out quickly. Five minutes later, there was a shootout in the streets.

Once again, John had a gun pointed at him from close range, and once again he escaped without injury. Previously it was because the assailant's gun had jammed. This time it was because the gunman showed mercy. He didn't shoot John, because they had been friends while John was in New York.

"Like I said, I've been blessed," John says with a smile. "It's weird to be liked and hated at the same time. The guy pointed the gun at me and shot the guy beside me. I remember he shot him right in the face. He could have shot me, too, but chose not to. I know his name, but don't want to say."

The anonymous shooter also put a bullet in the chest of another member of John's gang. John threw them both into another car, an old Crown Victoria, and sped off for the hospital. Those victims' lives were saved. Two months later, two other gang members were not as fortunate.

On October 28, 1991, Vietnamese teenagers Ty Nguyen and Chot Huynh were gunned down in Dorchester. Each man was shot in the chest from close range. Police immediately suspected the killings were gang related.

"I've been watching Asian gangs all over the world," detective Jim Goldman told the *Boston Globe*. "And I've never seen anything like the eighteen months I've been in Boston. The shootings are way out of proportion here."

The multiple homicides had attracted the attention of the police, and Chinatown's bosses and their gangs were no longer able to work in relative anonymity. There was definitely a war going on, and each combatant had a part to play. John's role was to differentiate between paranoia and justifiable caution, but when it came to protecting Bai Ming, it was better to be safe than sorry.

"A lot of us stayed in a house in Malden," John begins. "We'd stay in Chinatown until about four in the morning. Then maybe six or seven of us would leave and six or seven new guys would come in. Back home, guys would sit around, smoke weed, eat fruit, you know, good food, and come back and do it all over again. This was our job. We'd be watching for New York plates, and we'd write them down. Maybe a van from somewhere else shows up. Okay, who are they? Four or five guys show up in the restaurant. Okay, pull them aside.

Check their IDs. Why are they here? What do they want? It was almost like law enforcement, but that was the way we did it. Sometimes it broke out in stabbings or gun fights. Sometimes there was nothing. It was our way of protecting the area."

Oftentimes the area was also being watched by local law enforcement and the FBI. John says the police would sit in their cars and wait for the gang kids to drive by on their way to Chinatown. John would wave to them and then take up his post in the parking lot. The police would park nearby in an unconcealed stakeout. There were few, if any, secrets between the two sides. The gangs knew the police were there, and the police knew the gangs were involved in selling drugs and extorting money. From their vantage point, the police could see John directing kids to come and go. They witnessed the radio communications, and they followed the gang members to the gambling houses and the local businesses, but in most cases the police were powerless to do anything because the citizens and merchants of Chinatown were afraid to cooperate.

"At that point we did a lot of collecting from all the stores," John says euphemistically. "We'd collect from restaurants, video stores, jewelry stores, you name it. And in the Asian community, people were fine with that because they knew it was like having credit with a bank. The majority of them borrowed money to open their business, or to maintain their business. So, it was kind of like a financial institution inside of Chinatown. The people who wanted to open a business had to do something. So, they came and borrowed money, and they paid money back."

John's explanation refers to the common practice of Chinese and Vietnamese immigrants settling in Chinatown and borrowing money from the gang bosses to start up a business. The Asian immigrants couldn't get money from a bank, so they went to the tongs, which were business associations located in small and large neighborhoods. The tongs provided social and business services to members, and also acted as credit unions. It was all done legitimately and with beneficence, but rules within the tongs were often strictly enforced by gangs. The shop owners who borrowed money ended up owing the crime lords for the rest of their lives. They were victims of the system, but they acquiesced to its rules and handed over the money each month without much protest.

Occasionally, merchants would tire of being forced to hand over money for years on end. That's what police believe happened to David Eng, the owner of an Asian supermarket who turned up dead on the sidewalk just a few steps outside the Ping On headquarters in January of 1990. Eng was found in ten inches of snow with bullet wounds in his back and in the left side of his face. He had $5,000 in cash on him, so robbery was ruled out as a possible motive. No gun was found. No witnesses stepped forward. And no one was ever arrested for the killing.

"What we did," John explains, "is 'A' we made sure the streets were safe. 'B' we watched the gambling houses and made sure they couldn't get robbed, and 'C' we went around and made sure the businesses were safe. So we had a position to play, you know what I mean? The government, the police, everyone made us feel that we are bad people."

John Willis' mind never stops. He bounces from one observation or anecdote to a recollection or faded memory to a so-called philosophical truth in a matter of seconds. Through it all, he strictly adheres to the belief that while his life has not been a normal one, the degree of violence he's been involved in and surrounded by has been an appropriate show of discretion and even valor. Now, his intelligence is unquestionable, so perhaps it is because his racing mind never stops that he never quite lands on the mark. He never reconciles the contradiction he has lived nearly every day since Woping Joe brought him into the gang. In John's overactive mind, there are two worlds: the normal one in which violence is condemned, and the gang world in which violence is justified.

"Well, gangsters hurt gangsters," he says. "Morons hurt innocent people. So, if you and I both work on buildings and we're putting down high beams 150 feet in the air, and you fall off, you know what I say? 'You work a dangerous job.' And it's the same thing. If you're out here running around and you're involved in organized crime, and you're involved in collecting money, if something happens to you, you chalk it up to that's what you were involved in. If you're violent toward me, I'm going to be violent toward you. That's the way it is. There's been plenty of people killed. There's been plenty of people lost, but you know what? Again, it's like falling off that building. That's what you signed up for."

So, John looks back without regret, and certainly without remorse. His lips even curl upward just a bit when he recalls the day the Angel Boys from Texas came up to Boston and opened fire inside his Chinatown parking lot. John says, "The cars were all shot up. They looked like Swiss cheese."

Another potential shootout was avoided when a car came flying into the parking lot with its lights off. Guns were drawn immediately, but John ordered his gang to stand down. He recognized the car and was able to quickly discern that it was a friend of his driving it.

"They were just having fun," John says. "But that's how people get shot and killed. We didn't know what was going on. We were our own little police force, and we did what we had to do, you know what I mean? And at the head of the police force was Bai Ming. He was the guy, and that was it."

Bai Ming's ascension to power was not the result of a premeditated strategy. Rather, his success was due to the failure of others. Attrition and patience were his greatest allies. When Sky Dragon and Hun Suk fled from authorities to evade criminal charges, and another of Sky Dragon's top lieutenants, Michael Kwong, was killed in his Arlington, Massachusetts, restuarant, there were two men sitting atop the pyramid of organized crime in Chinatown: Bai Ming and Wayne Kwong.

Ming and Kwong were longtime partners and friends. They ran successful gambling dens together and faithfully served under Sky Dragon for years, but it appears Kwong had more ambition, and when he left Boston amid suspicion that he was behind the 1989 murder of Michael Kwong, he stumbled upon an opportunity.

Wayne Kwong escaped and hid out in San Francisco. In his absence, Ming usurped authority in Boston and began to cut

Kwong out of his share of the gambling operations. Kwong was upset, but he couldn't do anything about it, because he was still on the run and had to lie low. He was staying at one of the homes of San Francisco gang lord Peter Chong, and it was there that Kwong learned all about Tien Ha Wui, or "Whole Earth Society"—and that would be his opportunity and his motivation to kill Bai Ming.

Peter Chong first set foot in the United States in 1982 with the alleged intention of promoting Chinese opera. He did, in fact, sponsor entertainment tours through his New Paradise Investment company, but part of his promotional efforts included threatening people to buy tickets, forcing them onto buses, and taking them to the shows. Chong received a commission for each ticket sold. This led to Chong becoming involved in illicit gang activity, and eventually, to his leadership role in an organized crime gang in Northern California known as Wo Hop To.

By the late 1980s, Chong had begun to forge a relationship with another gang leader, Raymond Chow. After coming to the United States as a sixteen-year-old, Chow joined the Hop Sing Tong gang in San Francisco and ultimately seized control of it. Chow was a big heroin dealer, but he was arrested and jailed for armed robbery. When he got out of prison in 1989, he met Chong and the two gang leaders united their organizations.

This is when Kwong entered the picture. He managed to ingratiate himself into the hierarchy of Chong and Chow's newly formed gang. Chong effectively took Kwong under his wing. He put him up in a hotel for a while, paid his bills, and gave him walking-around money. The two almost had a falling-out when Kwong began staying at Chong's house. Chong apparently forgot to tell Kwong that he was going to set fire to the house, and Kwong ended up losing all his valuables in the blaze. But arson wasn't enough to slow the momentum of Tien Ha Wui.

Chong maintained his singular focus on uniting Asian gangs throughout America, and Kwong's arrival gave him the impetus to begin in Boston. Kwong wanted Bai Ming out of the way for his own purposes, and Chong was more than willing to help for his own greater one.

"Bai Ming is in the way over there," Kwong told Chong.

"Then kick him out," Chong replied. "Take care of him."

Assassination plans within Asian gangs tended to involve associates from a different city. So, Chong and Raymond Chow sent an underling to establish a foothold in Boston.

"The job was to take over the Boston town," Chow said. "To open a gambling place."

That underling may very well have been Dai Keung, because Chong would later tell his associates that the first man he sent in to Boston was killed. He didn't identify the victim, but admitted he was seeking revenge for the killing. He then instructed a young Hop Sing Tong member named Brandon Casey to go to Boston and kill Ming. Casey is also suspected of being the accomplice who helped set fire to Chong's own house.

The plan was simple. Casey would connect with a couple of Ghost Shadow members from New York, and the three hit men would spray bullets into a restaurant where Ming was eating. It would be reminiscent of the Golden Dragon

Massacre in San Francisco back in 1977, in which five people were killed and eleven others injured when members of one youth gang tried to kill members of a rival gang. Raymond Chow was among the intended victims, but he escaped unharmed. None of the victims were gang members. All five of the shooters were convicted. And still, Chow thought a copycat shooting was a viable plan.

On March 9, 1992, the killers picked up Kwong at his home in Randolph and drove to another house in Quincy, where they picked up a semiautomatic 9mm pistol and two other guns. Their next stop was at the China Pearl restaurant on Tyler Street in Chinatown. Kwong told them Ming would be eating at his favorite table on the second floor. He also told them that Ming wore a bulletproof vest, so they would have to shoot him in the head. However, when the shooters arrived, they saw a man they correctly assumed was an FBI agent get out of his car and walk toward the restaurant. The mission to kill Ming had to be aborted. So, they turned around and went back to Randolph. The next night, following Kwong's new orders, they went back to Chinatown intending to rob two bookmakers of more than $50,000 in cash. Again, the plan had to be aborted when they realized the police were following them. These incidents should have tipped off Casey and his cohorts that the police had some kind of heads-up that trouble was imminent, but they ignored the warning signs.

"The feds interviewed me," John recalls. "They knew I spoke for Ming. At that point, they were trying to share information to tell him that people were trying to kill him. We didn't think much of it. Figured they were just trying to get Ming to talk. They named different groups, and we looked into it. Thought it was nothing. But the feds had wiretaps, and the guys from New York were talking about the hit and setting it up, and that's how they got caught."

Only momentarily deterred each time he noticed a police presence, Casey waited for another opportunity to kill Ming. It came when Ming went to a wedding reception at the China Pearl. This time a sniper was positioned on a roof across the street.

"I know that there's a black guy the feds arrested on a rooftop," John says. "We were at the wedding, and Ming came out, and the guy was waiting to shoot him, but the feds arrested that guy."

Federal authorities had gotten wind of the plan to kill Ming because they were deeply entrenched in an effort to bring down Chong and Chow. They had surveillance on Chow for several months and learned that his devotion to criminal activity was incessant.

"After following him, he did nothing else but," FBI Special Agent Joe Davidson told the *San Francisco Chronicle*. "When the wire was up, that's all he did."

The FBI patiently followed Chow and baited him into unknowingly buying $100,000 of cocaine from a DEA agent. Now the feds had Chow, Chong, and Kwong on a variety of charges, including drug dealing, extortion, racketeering, and the attempted murder-for-hire of Bai Ming.

The indictments came down on March 16, 1992, one week after the second failed assassination attempt. Kwong was arrested on June 2 at his home in Randolph, and $25,000 in cash he had in the home was seized. Chow was picked up soon thereafter in San Francisco, but Chong made it safely to Hong Kong. That left only Kwong and Chow to take the fall, and Kwong decided it was best to cut a deal. Instead of receiving a minimum of fifteen years on racketeering charges, Kwong landed a five-year sentence. He pleaded guilty and testified against Chow.

Chow went to trial for suspicion of dealing heroin, money laundering, illegal gambling, arson, running a prostitution ring, and murder-for-hire, but Kwong's testimony lacked credibility, and the jury could not reach a verdict. It appeared Chow might be able to avoid prison time, but the San Francisco district attorney had wisely split Chow's case into separate trials. In a second trial, Chow was convicted on six counts of gun trafficking and sentenced to twenty-four years in prison.

Meanwhile, the Department of Justice spent eight years compiling enough legal evidence against Chong to convince China to extradite him back to the United States. When Chong arrived, he found Raymond Chow all too willing to testify against him. Chow was able to get his sentence reduced by telling a jury about the plan to kill Bai Ming and about Chong's significant role in the international heroin trade. Chow bragged from the witness stand, which seemed to make him more believable.

"If you're asking me which gang did I join," Chow testified, "I did not join any gang. I owned the gang. All those people who were walking the streets of the Bay Area, all of them were controlled by me."

Chong's trial in 2002 lasted eight weeks. He was found guilty of murder-for-hire, racketeering, extortion, and arson, and he was sentenced to fifteen years and eight months. For his cooperation, Chow was released from prison a year later. He had served eleven years of his twenty-four-year sentence.

"If you're going to catch the devil, you gotta go to hell," agent Davidson said. "You gotta deal with demons to get the head demon. You're not going to deal with priests or with schoolteachers."

Chong appealed his conviction, and in April of 2004, his lawyers filed a brief attempting to discredit Chow by calling him a career criminal and a liar. Perhaps to paint him in the worst light possible, the brief accused Chow of "owning a brothel in Pacifica staffed by girls as young as thirteen or fourteen years old."

That argument was not persuasive, but the Ninth U.S. Circuit Court of Appeals did ultimately overturn Chong's conviction on the charge of trying to kill Bai Ming. The reason given was that Chong never agreed to pay for the murder. Without an exchange of "anything of pecuniary value," the plan couldn't accurately be considered a murder-for-hire.

"There must be evidence that the hit men clearly understood they would receive something of pecuniary value in exchange for performing the solicited murderous act," the court ruled. "That evidence is lacking here."

The court overturned the conviction despite acknowledging and apparently understanding the hierarchy and the inner workings of a gang. It stated that money collected from criminal activities was used to pay underlings for specific missions. Brandon Casey testified himself that when he was asked to commit arson, he told a third party, "Peter Chong is going to pay real good."

The court heard the testimony of Oakland police sergeant Harry Hu stating that underlings would get their orders from senior members of the gang, but "normally they do not go all the way to the top, because the leaders insulate themselves, and foot soldiers do not need all the details of operations."

The court agreed that Chong caused the attempted murder-for-hire of Bai Ming, and in its ruling, the court further said: "Chong's underlings were commissioned by his lieutenants to travel from San Francisco to Boston for the purpose of killing Ming. Even if Chong did not give an explicit order to kill Ming, Chong agreed with Kwong's assessment that getting rid of Ming was essential for expanding the gang's presence to the East Coast. The record before us provides sufficient evidence from which a jury could have found that Chong or his coconspirators set in motion a series of events, resulting in his underlings traveling to Boston for the purpose of killing Bai Ming."

And still, the court overturned Chong's conviction.

The court was convinced that Casey did not enter into an agreement with Chong to kill Ming for several reasons: First, he had never met Chong. Second, Casey didn't know that he'd been sent to Boston to kill Ming until he got there. And finally, the government contended that Casey had been paid $100 to kill Ming, but Casey couldn't even recall if he'd been paid.

"Even if the hundred dollars could be sufficient consideration," the court said in its ruling, "the evidence does not

support the government's claim that this money was promised to Casey in return for murdering Bai Ming. Indeed,
Casey did not know the purpose for which he was being sent
to Boston before he left San Francisco…Casey knew the job
was dangerous and violent. He was aware before they left
that they were bringing guns to complete the task. However,
it was not until after Casey and the other underlings had
arrived in Boston and shortly before the murder attempt
that Kwong told Casey 'that we were there to kill someone. A
guy named Bai Ming.' None of this shows that Casey entered
into an agreement…with the Wo Hop To lieutenants that he
would kill Ming in return for some form of pecuniary consideration, as the statute requires."

Chong served only five years in prison. He was released
on July 29, 2008, at the age of sixty-five. His plan for the
Whole Earth Society never came to fruition, in large measure
because Bai Ming survived.

Bai Ming survived, but Ping On did not. With each transfer of power from Sky Dragon to Michael Kwong to Wayne
Kwong and Hun Suk, the overall structure of the gang weakened, until it finally ended up in the hands of Bai Ming, who
showed enough wisdom and guile to emerge from the power
struggle as the lone survivor, but who was ill-equipped to
lead.

"Bai Ming was a pretty hated man," a former gang member affirms. "His tactics and the way he does business, not
many people were fond of him. Nobody followed him. He
wasn't god. He wasn't god like Sky Dragon. He didn't have
that legacy. He was just a midlevel gangster. He didn't really fit

anywhere. He just filled the void. There were plenty of other people who were higher than Bai Ming when Sky Dragon was on the run. Everything just broke down. The whole outfit of Ping On crumbled. Bai Ming was just an interim Chinatown boss."

John Willis was there for the dissolution of Ping On, and he was there for the rise of Bai Ming. It didn't matter to John that Ming's business practices and surly personality made him unpopular. Ming was his boss, and John was loyal to him, just as he remained loyal to his brothers in the gang.

"When I was younger, there was people that had to go, you know what I mean? And I, I didn't, I never told my boss no. He told me to do something, I did it. Whatever he said, he said. That was it. There was no in between. We weren't there to make decisions. He was. That's just the way it happens. There was never 'no' involved. So even if you didn't like it, you did it."

And it certainly didn't matter whether the gang had the Ping On name anymore.

"It's not like we were printing T-shirts with Ping On written across our chests," John jokes.

However, the collapse of Ping On as a recognizable power was no laughing matter. It meant that Chinatown was up for grabs, and the first to make a move was John's good friend Ay-yat, who walked out of prison and tried to shoot his way to the top.

FIVE

"IT'S AN UNDERSTANDING that I've had since I was a little kid," John Willis explains. "You walk on this road, you're gonna see one of two things happen. You will either be killed or go to prison—that's just part of it. And again, I'll say it: I didn't choose this road. This is just the road that I'm on. You know what I mean? I didn't choose to one day wake up and have nowhere to live. I didn't choose to wake up and have no back, no family. You know what I mean? Then when I got this newfound family, they showed me respect. They helped me grow as a man."

The greatest influence on John as he was developing his own sense of morality and the principles by which he would live his life was Bai Ming. They were an odd couple: the white kid from Dorchester and the Chinese man emerging as the new godfather of Chinatown. But their relationship was symbiotic. Ming was happy to have the largest person in Chinatown as his bodyguard, and John got himself a father figure.

"Yes, I wanted to learn from him," John says. "He was very smooth in the things that he did, and that's how I learned. I learned how to treat people. Everything comes around in this world, and if you're going to do business, you have to do right business. Don't do bad business unless other people dictate that. If someone does something and you have to teach them a lesson, then that's what you're gonna do. Don't be afraid to stomp on people who need to be stomped on. And that's just the way it goes in life. This is not a life for the fainthearted people. This is a life that you live if you're ready to go to the next level. But really be prepared for that. Don't talk about it. Do it."

Ming, whose real name is Tan Ngo, is of Chinese descent but was born in Vietnam. His right leg was badly injured when he stepped on a land mine left over from the war. He was taken to a hospital, but the leg was never properly cared for, and he would forever walk with a limp. Thus, the nickname Bai Ming, which means "crippled Ming." He left Vietnam and landed first in San Francisco, where some of his family had already settled. He eventually moved to Boston, where he married and had children, and where he went to work for Sky Dragon.

At first, Ming viewed John as little more than a curiosity. He never tired of hearing a perfect Chinese accent coming out of John's round Caucasian face, but the novelty of John's talent would only take him so far. He would have to earn the rest. And he did. Ming soon learned that John was the most reliable and trustworthy member of his gang. The others could be wild and unpredictable, but John was dedicated to the cause and he had a strong desire to please, and those two attributes made him dependable.

So, Ming effectively adopted him. John moved into Ming's house in Watertown and spent nearly every day with him for several years. John was Ming's traveling companion, protégé, enforcer, and bodyguard, and he was expected to be a bodyguard without a girlfriend.

"You know, his whole thing was, 'What do you need a girlfriend for?'" John recalls. "He'd say, 'Establish your life first, and then think about the girls. Think about everything else. How you protecting me if you're worrying about where she's going?' You know, that's his type of attitude. And back then in the late '80s, early '90s, it was a very violent Chinatown. There were a lot of murders, a lot of, you know, stabbings, a lot of gunfights, different things. You know, we would go to different states, different places, and you'd have to be aware of your surroundings. If you weren't, then you'd end up dead, or maybe get him killed."

So, in the mornings, John would check the car to see whether it had been tampered with overnight. He'd look underneath and pop the hood, looking for explosives. Once he was satisfied the car was safe, he'd get behind the wheel and think for a moment: "Am I willing to die today?" And the answer was always the same. John believed he owed his life to Ming, because Ming was the leader of the gang that saved him and accepted him. Ming also gave John what he craved most: respect. So, every morning John turned the key and started the engine.

"I'm white, but I was raised by Chinese," John says. "These people took care of me. They basically gave me life, and I live that life. I'm not some white kid saying, 'Hey, I hung around with a bunch of Asian guys, and that makes me different.' The truth is, I am different, because my beliefs are different. I lived that culture. I need that culture because I respect it. I live it, and I hold my head up every day because of it. And that's just the way it is with me. I was a young kid with nobody. I had nothing. I grew up in this life. So, I admired their culture. I took their culture as my own. I'm grateful for everything I learned. It's about my 'face.' The worst thing you can do to me is insult my face, insult my intelligence, insult my culture. These people raised me. I had nothing."

It's a debt of gratitude that runs deep in John. He speaks often and passionately about loyalty and respect. He believes he understands what they mean, and that he lives those principles unwaveringly. He believes loyalty and respect are given the greatest importance in the Chinese culture, and perhaps even more so in the Chinese gang culture.

"In America, we don't grow up with the same camaraderie," John explains. "I know when I'm out there that I'm willing to die for this guy with me, and he's prepared to die for me. In America, you might be willing to get into a fistfight for someone, but after that he's on his own. We grew up with people trying to kill us, chasing us with machetes, chopping off arms, and you were there with your brother. You knew you couldn't leave him no matter what. If you did, you were a real piece of shit. That was more important to me than any school could teach me, that sense of brotherhood. I lived that."

Of course, in order to believe as firmly as he does that the Chinese culture he was immersed in is deeply rooted in respect and loyalty, he must ignore the violence that commands the respect, and the fear that induces the loyalty, as well as the hypocrisies and betrayals that he witnessed on a daily basis. He knows what it's like to be with friends who ran when trouble started. He's aware of guys who cooperated with police. He knows the system is rigged so the biggest, strongest, and meanest guys get the most respect, but he ignores those truths. When he marvels about how easy it was to walk into any restaurant in Chinatown "even if we had a hundred people," and they could all eat without paying, because "our boss would take care of it one way or another," he ignores the obvious fact that there is no respect being given to the bullied restaurant owner. John is willing to ask the relevant question, but dismisses the obvious answer.

"We had respect among people," John says. "They respected us or feared us. There's a fine line between both. We're out there. We lived a certain way, but we also earned our respect. Did we put fear in these people? I don't know. To this day, I don't know the true answer, but that's the way it goes."

John learned by watching Ming. He was with him nearly every day. Ming was the most successful man John had ever met, and John was determined to learn from him as much as he could. One of his first lessons came at a Japanese restaurant. The chef was playfully tossing food in a hibachi when a shrimp tail went astray and hit Ming. The chef apologized, and Ming accepted, but only after he ordered the chef to put his hand inside the hot hibachi. The chef obediently did as he was told, and Ming smiled while the chef's hand was badly burned. John watched, and he learned.

"That was just to let the chef know he was playing with the wrong people," John explains. "Ming was like that. He could be a real mean guy if he wanted to be. He didn't play around. That's the way it's supposed to be. That's what you have to be about, or else people won't respect you, and do what you tell them to do. If you have no standing, you have nothing."

Ming certainly had standing in Chinatown and beyond. His rise to power may not have been premeditated, but it was real nonetheless. And he had real and many enemies. Some of them tried to burn Ming alive. He and his family, and John, were asleep in their home one night, unaware that someone was outside pouring gasoline all along the perimeter of the house and on the cars parked outside. John was the first to wake up when he heard the sound of breaking glass and the loud squeal of spinning tires. The assailants had thrown a Molotov cocktail at the house and then sped away. John rushed outside and saw a small fire burning.

"They missed," he says. "Thank God. They hit the staircase beside the house, and it didn't ignite the gasoline."

After that, John returned to saying daily prayers. He had begun the practice while running with the gangs in New

York. They would light incense and put punk reeds in a bowl of rice, bow their heads, and say a few words of peace before they went out to rob gambling houses. They were praying for a safe return, and John figured it was once again a good idea. He also took to wearing a bulletproof vest from time to time. Ming did as well, and around his waist, Ming always wore a beaded sash that had been blessed. They were aware of the danger, and it followed them everywhere.

"Ming is originally from San Francisco," John begins another story. "We went out there, and we were eating in a restaurant. A guy comes in and starts arguing with my boss's 'brother.' When the guy goes outside, another kid runs out and shoots him five times. And the guy didn't die! He was so high on PCP, he didn't even go down. You could see five holes in him!"

Before the police arrived, John and Ming hurried away and stepped inside a pet store across the street. Peering through the clear water of a large fish tank, they watched like excited kids at Christmas as the police and ambulances arrived.

"And the really crazy part," John continues, "is I talked to that kid who did the shooting probably about three weeks later, and he told me he tried to shoot the guy again. He put the gun to his head and it didn't go off! He said to me, 'I not try to kill him no more. God wants him to live.'"

Back in Boston's Chinatown, Ming and John were running a successful business, and going mostly undetected by law enforcement. There was one blemish on John's record when he was arrested for stealing a car and getting involved in a high-speed chase, but he spent only one night in jail. He was released and returned to doing Ming's bidding until early 1992, when John was charged with extortion and kidnapping. He pleaded guilty to lesser charges of attempted extortion and containment, and was given a ten-year sentence. He served only eighteen months at the South Bay House of Correction and enjoyed every minute of it.

"That was like being locked up with all your friends," John says. "My cellmate was my boy E.T., and the guards were all guys I grew up with in Dorchester."

While John was in jail, he spent a lot of time thinking about his friend Chay Giang, whom he had watched die in a parking lot. Giang's murder affected John like no other death before. He wasn't angry as he had been when his brother died, and he wasn't depressed, as he had been when his mother died; nor was he apathetic as he had been when he had previously seen people get killed. Giang's death caused John to finally look more closely at the senselessness of the violence that surrounded him. A few tense words led to a heated argument, and then *bang!*—someone was dead. John held that someone's limp body in his arms, and in that moment, he changed a little bit. He wasn't aware of it at the time, and no one would have noticed, because nothing about his day-to-day life would change until he went to prison. But jail gave him the time and opportunity to finally address what had happened, and the change became more perceptible. Giang's death made John question what he was doing with his life, and he made the conscious choice to change directions. John stepped out of prison in the fall of 1993, and began selling heroin.

"My boss [Ming] always said don't sell drugs," John recalls. "He said the problems that come from selling drugs are problems you don't want to face. Smartest thing he ever said. But you get blinded by money sometimes. The money was real good, and I was young. So, the money kind of influenced my decisions as far as selling drugs. I never did it in Chinatown, though. I never did it around any of my people."

John didn't start with small deals and work his way up to larger ones. He didn't dabble in marijuana before advancing to Ecstasy, cocaine, or heroin. He went big right from the start. He knew who the hard-core narcotics suppliers were, and he had the acumen to connect the dots among dealers and buyers to bring the enterprise to a mass scale. He didn't move from weed to coke to heroin. He dealt in all three simultaneously.

"China White was the best," John says, referring to one of the purest forms of heroin responsible for hundreds of deaths in the early '90s. "I remember the first time people asked me about it was when I was in jail. I didn't know what it was. So, when I got out, the first thing I said to my guy was, 'What's up with the China White?' And then in California, I had some good brothers out there, and they set it up and brought me a kilo of the stuff. I didn't know what to do. What am I gonna do with a kilo of heroin?"

John figured it out. It took a while, though. The first time he helped pack the heroin, he didn't wear gloves or a mask. That was a rookie mistake, because the heroin was so strong, it seeped into his pores.

"I was getting borderline high off this stuff, and didn't even realize it," John says. "So never again, y'know. My brother died due to cocaine use. So for me it was just something I would just never involve myself in. I've been around it, but I never, never touched it. Never will. It's a weakness. When you do drugs, you're hiding or running from something."

Just a dealer, and not a user, John coordinated the pick-ups and drop-offs using big trucks and black duffel bags. His group sold large quantities of marijuana throughout Canada and the United States. Most of the pot came from California. There was British Canadian marijuana known as the B.C. Beast. That sold for upward of $2,800 a pound. The hydro-weed known as "Arizona" actually came from California, and John remembers selling that for between $4,000 and $6,000 a pound. His dealers also supplied the Cambodian gangs in Lowell, Massachusetts, with whatever they needed, and they brought Ecstasy wherever there was a demand.

"Ecstasy," he says, "was pretty big in the early '90s. And China White is always big, you know what I mean?"

John did all this without involving Bai Ming, because he knew Ming would have disapproved. It was the beginning of John's transition from being Ming's right-hand man to being his own man. With Ming, there was only so far John could rise, only so much money he could make. Ming took care of him with a salary that approached $100,000 per year, but John was starting to make that much in a matter of weeks. John stayed loosely attached to Bai Ming, but he was effectively bouncing like an independent contractor among several groups. He was making a lot of money, but to keep his drug dealing a secret from Ming, John didn't spend much of it—at first. He simply collected the cash and set it aside. He saved hundreds of thousands of dollars until he just couldn't resist temptation any longer. He bought a house in South Carolina, three cars, and a boat.

Ming took notice. The more lavish John's lifestyle became, the more obvious it became to Ming where the money was coming from. Ming wasn't upset. There was no official falling-out. He didn't demand John cut him in on the action. He simply and slowly distanced himself from John. Ming was many things, but he was not a drug dealer. John, however, was. And he was a good one, and one who lived without regret.

"I see it as a business," John explains. "If you told me we were going to sell lollipops and make this kind of money, I'm gonna find a way to make lollipops. I like the idea of taking care of myself and making money. I like to do business because, 'A' I like to tell me what I'm doing, nobody else; and 'B' the money side of it is, if you give me the best deal I can get, I can give everybody else the best deal they can get."

But Ming was right about drugs bringing on a lot of problems. Ming's philosophy was to stay inside Chinatown, where everything was insulated. He stuck to operating the gambling dens, which the police tended to ignore, and to collecting from local business owners, who knew it was best not to talk to the police. It was a safe and conservative approach to criminal activity, but the ceiling for profitability was too low for John's tastes. He stepped outside Chinatown, where opportunities were unlimited but where encounters with the police were far more commonplace.

John recalls the time he was in a large warehouse full of bales of marijuana. He and a few other guys were loading the bales onto a truck when John noticed the guy next to him wearing a badge on his belt.

"What's with the guy with the badge?" John asked a couple of his Italian friends.

"Don't worry about him," John was told. "He's a New York City detective. Been working with us for years."

Two weeks later, John says that same detective was sitting in his unmarked squad car when John went over to him and delivered $200,000 in cash. It was part of doing business, but as John got further away from Boston, he found himself further away from the bonds of loyalty among his brothers that he had grown to respect so much. It was disheartening to learn his friends in the drug-dealing world couldn't always be trusted.

"I'm not a thief," John declares. "I don't like them. I would respect you if you walked up and took something from a guy. That's your business. You took something from him. Fuck him! I got respect for you, because you took it from him. If you go and steal something, that's a big difference. If you sneak thief it, that's garbage. I've had things stolen from me, and obviously, the most important thing isn't getting the stuff back; it's finding out who stole it.

"This is a true look at me," John continues. "I don't expect anything back. What I do expect is for a man to be honest about his way. I don't care what you do in your life. Don't respect me and then go over and disrespect that man there. That means the respect you gave me means nothing, because you're not a respectful human being. Everything you brought to me is a lie.

"My philosophy on life is not something I learned from books; it comes from my life experience. I learned that when I give, I get back more. When I give a little, I get a little more. I do it because it's the right thing to do."

Black and white. Right and wrong. John can talk about it for hours. There are no moral dilemmas, no hypothetical situations that don't have quick, obvious answers for how to handle them. There is no hesitation when he speaks about what he's done, why he's done it, and why he'd do it again. His life's code is impenetrable.

"I'm on Lansdowne Street one time," John says, referring to the one-way street behind Fenway Park in Boston. "My younger brother, a tough kid, he's not the type of kid to hit you with a bottle, but he was going to court for fighting with the bouncers at a club there. One of the bouncers got stitches, because he was hit with a Champagne bottle. I know who hit him with the bottle. It was another one of my boys. He's an asshole. He does shit like that. I talked to the bouncer."

"Your boy hit me," the bouncer told John.

"No, he didn't," John responded. "I know he didn't do it."

"Yes, he did," the bouncer argued. "I saw him. My boys seen it, too."

"Look," John said, as he began to explain the situation to the bouncer who was nearly as large as he was, "you're in a dark club with a bunch of Asians. They all look the same. Anyway, how about you don't go to court? I'll give you a couple of thousand dollars and pay your hospital bills, and we'll end all this."

John thought it was a fair offer, but the bouncer refused and continued to argue his point that the kid should pay for hitting him with a bottle.

"All right," John said finally. "You don't have to do anything, but I will tell you this: If you're going to work outside here, invest in a bulletproof vest and a helmet. Enjoy your life. That's it. It's over with."

John poked his finger in the bouncer's chest and walked away. About forty minutes later, John received a call from the manager of the club who begged him to reconsider.

"I spoke to your guy," John said flatly. "I gave him an opportunity to do the right thing. There's nothing more to talk about. I wouldn't put him at the front door anymore, if I were you."

To reinforce his point, John went to the Roxbury courthouse where his "boy" was going before the judge in a pretrial hearing. The bouncer and a couple of his friends were standing outside the district attorney's office when John arrived.

"I see these big black guys standing outside the DA's office," John recalls. "I go right up to them, and I looked at every one of them. Those kids went in and told the judge they couldn't identity any of the Asian kids. To me, they did the right thing. The first kid didn't do the right thing until he was persuaded, but I still told my boy to go and give him the money for his hospital bill, and be a gentleman about it. I'm not God. I'm not the judge or the jury. I'm just all about the resolution."

John has no patience for fools, and a fool is anyone who can't see the obvious, anyone who hesitates to behave or react in a clear and decisive manner. For John, life is unambiguous. Knowing how to handle a situation is simply a matter of knowing who you are, and staying true to that and to those you love. He looks at his own life and believes the path God put him on when he was fifteen years old was undeniable. So, he had no choice but to take it. It's difficult for John to understand when people choose an alternate route, and it happened many times in drug deals gone wrong. As an example, John recalls the time he brought $29,000 cash with him to make a purchase, but he could sense early on that he was being set up.

"It was stupid money," John says, implying that it wasn't a lot of money. "But it's money you shouldn't steal from your friends. This guy has made thousands of dollars every week, and now he's out. Now he has to fend for himself. No more business for him. He had to sit and watch everybody else make money."

In a matter of just a few months in 1993, John had stepped out of prison and into a world made for big-time players in the drug business. Almost overnight he had become someone who doesn't think $29,000 is a lot of money to make or lose in a day. He began gambling large amounts of money in the dens, winning and losing with the same carefree attitude. Winning only added to his already large pile of money, and if he lost, he'd make all of it back and then some on the next big deal.

John happened to be in a gambling den a few days before Christmas of '93 when news spread quickly that Sky Dragon had been indicted. The charges against him were racketeering, conspiracy, illegal gambling, smuggling illegal immigrants, and violence in the aid of racketeering and loansharking. John stopped playing mahjongg long enough to notice the look of concern on Bai Ming's face. It surprised John, because he hadn't yet deduced what Ming had instantly figured out. The only reason the authorities indicted Sky Dragon was because they knew where he was, and once they arrested him, a lot of people, especially Ming, could be in trouble.

Ming was correct. Less than three weeks after the indictment came down, Sky Dragon was stopped by immigration officers at a Hong Kong airport. He surrendered both himself and the $150,000 in cash he was carrying. Hours later, a hundred FBI agents conducted a series of raids at more than two dozen residences in the Boston area. When their sweep was concluded, nine members of Ping On had been arrested and six others were still being pursued. The seventeen-count indictment against the defendants stated:

"The [Ping On] enterprise acted to protect itself by intimidation, violence and threats of violence against other criminal groups and individuals which it perceived as a threat to its territory."

Bai Ming and John were not among those indicted because the alleged crimes took place before even Ming was intimately involved in Ping On's activities. Meanwhile, Sky Dragon could not be extradited to the United States because Hong Kong's treaty with the U.S. does not recognize racketeering offenses. It didn't take long, however, for the charges against Sky Dragon to escalate to include a conspiracy to commit murder charge. His former henchman Kwok-Wah Chan was prepared to testify against Sky Dragon regarding the assassination attempt on Dai Keung and Chao Va Meng in 1988. The Chinese government consented to turn Sky Dragon over to be tried only on the murder conspiracy charge. He was brought back to Boston to stand trial, but Sky Dragon agreed to plead guilty when prosecutors offered to recommend an eight-year sentence. That deal fell through, however, when U.S. District Judge Nathaniel Gorton dismissed the plea, stating a ninety-six-month sentence was not sufficient punishment.

A trial was held in the summer of 1996, during which evidence was presented that proved under Sky Dragon's leadership, the Ping On gang extorted money from restaurants and gambling dens, bribed police officers, and attempted to kill Keung and Meng in a Chinatown parking lot on December 29, 1988. Sky Dragon was convicted and sentenced to fifteen years and eight months in prison. Additionally, he was fined $175,000. He served eleven years and was released from a Rye, New York, prison in 2007. He never again set foot in Chinatown, opting instead to return to Hong Kong, where he enjoys a much simpler life as a wine importer.

Authorities championed Sky Dragon's imprisonment as a law-enforcement success story because it had left a void in Chinatown's gang power structure. But that victory took years to attain. Sky Dragon initially left Boston in 1989. He was extradited in 1994 and convicted on July 29, 1996. In those seven years, the godfather of Chinatown role he vacated was filled by the likes of Michael Kwong, Wayne Kwong, and

Bai Ming. Sky Dragon's departure and ultimate conviction weakened Ping On, but that only meant it was vulnerable to attack. What law enforcement perceived as a battle won merely opened the door to more violence by a small, disorganized group of criminals staking out a claim inside and outside Chinatown. Once controlled by a singular power, Chinatown would become the Wild West, and the cowboys wearing black hats went by the names of Ay-yat, Phong Ly, David Yee, William Chan, and yes, even White Boy John.

"At the end," an FBI special agent told the *Boston Globe*, "nobody was left standing."

SIX

JOHN WILLIS should be dead. After all, death is typically what happens to a man who has a gun pointed at him and the trigger pulled at close range. But that day in the rain-soaked parking lot with Giang, the gun jammed! And in the gunfight in North Station, the gunman who had a clear shot turned out to be an old acquaintance of John's. And he didn't fire! Other gunmen in other gunfights did fire, but missed their mark. Each time, John was lucky to survive; just as he was when the arsonist tried to burn Ming's house while they slept; just as he was when he awoke from a diabetic coma; and just as he was when he fell asleep at the wheel and crashed his car into a mountain.

"THE GRACE of God saved me that time," John states emphatically. "I was up for a couple of days partying. We were waiting for things to get done, and I had a decent amount of drugs in the car—taking them back to Boston from New York. In Connecticut, I fell asleep and crashed the car." John's next memory is of himself waking up and flying through the air. He had been ejected from the car, but he has no logical explanation as to how. The windshield wasn't broken. The doors remained shut, and the sunroof was too small for him to fit through, yet there he was: flying through the air.

"God picked me up and threw me out of the car," John swears. "It was crazy! The car ended up tipped up on a rock with my friend, Richie, underneath it. He was okay, too."

The next thing John remembers seeing was an 18-wheeler rolling up on the scene. Damn! John had to act quickly. He barked orders to Richie in Chinese. Richie crawled out from under the car, grabbed the keys from the ignition, and raced to the trunk. He reached in and grabbed a crowbar and the large duffel bag of cocaine. He ran off into the darkness and buried the drugs. Meanwhile, John flagged down the truck driver and then distracted him with a long tale of what had happened, though he never mentioned there was another passenger in the car. Finally, Richie returned with another concocted story claiming to be disoriented and not knowing why he had wandered off. When the police arrived,

John explained that he had fallen asleep at the wheel, and because there was no reason to suspect otherwise, there was no additional investigation. John and Richie were treated and released from a nearby hospital, and a few days later their friends from New York went to the accident scene and recovered the drugs. It was yet another brush with death that John lived to tell about, and with so many near-death experiences, John is asked if he believes God has kept him alive for a greater purpose.

"I always think about that," John admits before rejecting the notion. "No, I don't think there's a greater purpose, but every day there's a conversation with someone, and you can take something from that individual. The day you think you're beyond learning is the day you realize how stupid you are. That's the truth. I learn from everybody."

The question about a greater purpose was intended to imply that perhaps God was keeping John alive so he could do something good with his life, maybe even make amends for all his crimes and violence. Was there a chance God wanted him to turn his life around and help others instead of hurting them? But John interpreted the question differently, as if the supposed purpose that God intended would be for him to achieve more success, make more money, and have a happier life. His response speaks to extreme levels of ego and self-interest, but even more than that, it divulges his complete lack of remorse. John regrets nothing, and believes he has nothing for which to make amends.

"I'm square with God," John asserts. "I believe in heaven and I'm going there. To be honest, in my opinion, we're living in hell today. The things that go on in this world today, God didn't make the world for this to happen. In my view, he gave the devil his due. Go ahead do what you can do, and those who roll that way, there's your hell on earth. What happens after that is a different picture."

And the picture John paints is one in which a protective and loving God is leading him down a singular path. For John still believes that when he was fifteen years old, starving, scared, and freezing, it was God who gave him a way out; it was God who led him to Woping Joe and a family with the Ping On gang. It's interesting, then, considering John believes in heaven and hell, that it never crosses his mind that it was the devil he was following.

So, it may have been God that plucked John from the vehicle, carried him through the air, and placed him safely back on the ground, or it may have been luck. In fact, God and good fortune may be equally responsible for extricating John from myriad close calls, but he owes his survival to his patient study and his early understanding that he needed to be an ardent observer of his surroundings. John Willis is many things. Chief among them are student and communicator.

"John's talent was knowing how to word it and phrase it in a way to make people understand the logic of the system," former gang member David Yee offers. "When we needed to extort or collect on a debt, he was the go-to person. Whatever he decided, if it was not to lay a finger, then the softer side of his demeanor would come out. He spoke nicely and eloquently. He didn't need to flex his muscles. He wasn't a total devil. He has a softer side to him. And after a while, the soft threats were all he needed."

David Yee was sixteen years old in 1992, and for young Asian kids at that time Chinatown was like Rush Week for college fraternity pledges. Yee was recruited by several different gangs, and after flitting around like a fly looking for something rotten to land on, he finally joined the Ghost Shadows. His gang of choice made him John's rival, yet when Yee was being threatened by members of John's crew, it was John who stepped in as the mediator.

"It was all about the money," Yee explains. "Not so much the power. The money, the success, is what really drives him. His motives, his end goal in life, is pure business. When he was younger, it was all about respect. Once he built that off the local gangs in the Asian community, he was on a roll. It fueled his personality. He was the go-to man. He intimidated a lot of people. Big white guy. And when the Chinese guys respect him, everyone else would be petrified of him."

John was a leader who didn't like followers. He was all about business, and he preferred to take care of business himself. So, with the exception of a few guys he trusted and needed to help him carry out his drug business, John worked alone. Ming remained his boss for all things related to protection and collection, but in matters outside of Ming's purview, John was fast becoming his own boss. That, too, helped him survive in an ever-changing Chinatown. There were new gang alliances being forged and shattered seemingly overnight, and each time new friends returned to being old foes there was danger. John saw it coming and was able to deftly navigate through the new and treacherous minefields on the streets of Chinatown.

The first threat came from Phong Ly, an ethnic Chinese who emigrated from Vietnam in 1981. Phong Ly, who had struck up a friendship with Ay-yat while the two were in jail together, tried to position himself in the hierarchy of Chinatown, first by going to work for Ming, and then by branching out on his own. Phong Ly tried to recruit John, Woping Joe, Yee, William Chan, and others, but John kept to himself, Woping Joe and Yee followed Ay-yat, and only William went along with Phon Ly.

"Phong Ly built up an army with William," Yee explains, "and they started some gambling dens. Ay-yat didn't like that, not because he was trying to make money, but because of the disrespect. Like, 'Who the fuck are you?' So, Ay-yat had a couple of his associates gun him down."

PHONG LY was one of thousands of ethnic Chinese who emigrated from Vietnam in the late 1970s and early '80s. He made his way from Sacramento, California, to Boston, where he was arrested and convicted of shooting two restaurant employees during an attempted robbery. While in prison, he met and befriended Ay-yat, but soon after their respective releases, the two criminals had a falling-out. Police believed Phong Ly was killed because he stabbed one of Ay-yat's associates. David Yee says it was a much smaller offense that got Phong Ly killed.

"They were friends," Yee says. "But when they both came to Boston, Phong Ly said something stupid that Ay-yat didn't like. Ay-yat had taken care of him in jail when Phong Ly didn't have anybody else."

The penalty for saying "something stupid" to Ay-yat was death at the hands of two gunmen. Phong Ly, who was engaged to be married, spotted his two assassins on the streets of Chinatown and began running. It was just after three o'clock in the afternoon on a warm August day in 1994. Witnesses watched two Asian males with their guns drawn chasing Phong Ly down Kneeland Street and onto Tyler Street. Sweating profusely and breathing heavily, Phong Ly ran back to his job at Miss Lin's Employment Agency. It was located in the basement of an apartment building on Tyler Street, and Phong Ly probably thought he'd be safe surrounded by a dozen witnesses. He thought wrong. He only got as far as the doorway to the building when the gunmen fired six shots. By the time police arrived, Phong Ly was already dead.

His fiancée quickly learned of his murder and rushed to the scene, crying uncontrollably. She told police she had no idea who would want to kill Phong Ly or why. She said he was a good man who had been helping to support her twelve-year-old daughter. As she spoke with investigators just a few yards from Phong Ly's covered body, she noticed a wedding party slowly walking past the yellow tape and into the Golden Palace restaurant, where a reception was being held. Her own wedding invitations never made it into the mail.

The execution of Phong Ly did not sit well with Ming. Although it's true Phong Ly was operating independently, he remained one of Ming's lieutenants and paid Ming a share of the profits from his gambling dens. Ming was livid that Ay-yat would dishonor him by killing one of his men. The FBI believes Ming retaliated for Phong Ly's murder by killing one of Ay-yat's lieutenants. The body of twenty-six-year-old Hai Bo Lei was found on the side of Hampstead Road in Salem, New Hampshire, on March 30, 1995. Lei, a known associate of Ay-yat who went by the nickname Chicken Paul, had been shot several times and strangled. His badly beaten body was left to bleed out. No one was ever charged with the murder and it remains unsolved.

Ay-yat was finally arrested in October of 1995. FBI agents stopped him as he drove to dinner at a restaurant in Revere. He was charged with conspiracy to murder Phong Ly. Police said Ay-yat and his henchmen had failed in an earlier attempt when the weapons didn't fire. So, Ay-yat acquired new firearms and obsessively plotted the murder, including an escape route down Tyler Street. He might have gotten away with it, but one of his trusted followers, Qiang Chen Bing, cooperated with investigators and testified before a grand jury.

"A couple of individuals gunned him down," Yee explains. "They got caught and one of them basically turned on Ay-yat. His ever-trusting right-hand man, San Jai, meaning Snake Boy! He ratted him out to save his own hide. That's how he got indicted. Snake Boy is from New York. Part of Ghost Shadows. Ay-yat's right-hand man."

Qiang Chen Bing pleaded guilty to his part in the shooting and was sentenced to ten years in prison. The other shooter, Nhut Hoang Nguyen, was picked up by Royal Canadian Mounted Police in Toronto and returned to Massachusetts. He also pleaded guilty and was sentenced to twelve years in prison. Ay-yat admitted to being the mastermind of the murder plot, and after police found evidence of his heroin trafficking, extortion, and jewelry store robberies, he also pleaded guilty to those crimes, and in April of 1998 he was sentenced to a minimum of twenty-two years in jail.

Finally, Ay-yat's reign of terror was over. Police considered him to be the most dangerous Vietnamese gangster for the better part of a decade. He had been convicted of the Lowell jewelry store robbery in 1987 that left Mon Ly in a coma. Then, after being sentenced to eighteen years in prison, he was placed in a minimum-security prison in Shirley, Massachusetts. Thirteen days after his transfer there, he simply walked away from a work detail and vanished. He fled to Canada, where police claim he brought in $100,000 a week in extortion money and pulled a jewelry store heist in Calgary in 1990 in which he got away with more than $500,000 in jewelry. They say he orchestrated that robbery by cell phone from his car. Ay-yat was finally arrested in 1991 for the nightclub shootout in Toronto, but he wasn't convicted. So, he lasted out on the streets until he was caught in connection with the murder of Phong Ly.

Chinatown was changing. The relatively peaceful extortion and gambling days led by Sky Dragon were long gone, and now the most violent Chinese and Vietnamese gang leaders who replaced Sky Dragon were being toppled either by their own internal wars or by external forces like the police. One by one, they all found their way either to the grave or to prison.

William, who had teamed up with Phong Ly, was arrested a year after Phong Ly's death and charged with carrying a concealed weapon into the East Ocean City Restaurant on Beach Street. It was after three o'clock in the morning, and William was with a dozen other men demanding to be served alcohol. That was merely a bump in the road that led to a longer stay in prison, because police started watching him more closely. In fact, they watched him sell heroin from November of 1995 to January of 1996. William eventually pleaded guilty and was sentenced to forty months in prison.

So, with Ay-yat and William both in prison, and Phong Ly dead and buried, Ming and John faced fewer and fewer challengers to their power in Chinatown. Ming continued running his extortion and collection business, along with a few gambling dens, and John expanded his drug business.

"What I do as far as the drug side of things," John says, "I don't do in Chinatown. I did it away from Chinatown. So, that would be my personal business. My boss never wanted to sell drugs. He'd tell you straight up, 'Don't sell drugs. Brings too many problems.' And that's the way it was when I was a kid. I just followed what he said, but then as you grow older, you step outside, and you do what you do to make your money."

No longer content to hide his success, John bought a bright yellow Porsche convertible. He loved to rev the engine while speeding through Chinatown and the Boston suburbs. He shared his newfound wealth generously, bought diamond jewelry and watches, and dined at expensive restaurants nearly every night. These were good times for John Willis!

"I went to a big Japanese restaurant in Brookline a while back with this Russian girl," John begins. "It was a nice place. They had the rice paper doors, and the waiter says, 'Please take your shoes off.' Well, we had been at the beach all day and had flip-flops and sandals with sand on our feet, so I said, 'Do you mind if we don't take the shoes off?'"

The manager of the restaurant knew John personally, and was very aware of John's reputation, and he told the waiter, who was Chinese, not Japanese, not to make an issue about the shoes. The waiter obeyed, but very quietly and in Chinese asked why "this guy and his bitch don't have to take their shoes off." It wasn't said quietly enough, however, and once again John's ability to speak Chinese was underestimated. He overheard the comment, and he seethed while deciding how to handle the obvious affront. He tried to remain calm, but after John and his girl had been seated, the waiter bent over to deliver the drinks. John grabbed his girlfriend's shoe, which was a Croc with a hard, two-inch-thick base, and he cracked the waiter on the side of the face with it.

"You should watch your mouth before you talk," John scolded quietly and in Chinese. Then he split the waiter's lip open with another smack to the face. The waiter ran to the kitchen, and the manager tried to intervene.

"Please, Mr. John," the manager pleaded. "We don't want any trouble."

"I didn't start this trouble," John said. "Your waiter did by disrespecting us."

"He doesn't know you, Mr. John."

"Why should that matter?" John continued. "You think it's all right for him to call people 'bitch' because they don't understand the language?"

"Please, please, no more trouble. We will bring you free food. Free drinks. Whatever you want."

"I don't want to drink with you," John replied. "I want you to understand that person was wrong. He was rude. God forbid that was my mother!"

There are countless incidents like that as John traversed between his two worlds: the gang culture and normal society. Each time a situation exploded into something uncommonly combative, it was about respect—or more precisely, the perceived lack of it. Unapologetically, John defends the specific choices of his life with a general philosophy. He seems to desperately want his worldview to be understood.

"I think anybody out there who's been on the street ten or twenty years, people should respect you," John explains. "We're out there. We've been though the wars and the fights, and the killing. They should give us the due respect. Everyone will tell you that we're villains, but we're no different than a bunch of guys getting together to perform a task. That's what we did, and we respect each other. We did things that not everybody did. Is it normal to be carrying around pistols? No. Is it normal to smack somebody and break their head open because they did something? No, it's not normal. Unfortunately, that's the way it is. I'm thankful that I was taught a culture, and I was thankful that I was part of something. Yeah, there's violence, but that's a part of life."

Violence *is* a part of life, but while most people try to avoid it, John frequently sought it out. In fact, he seemed to take advantage of people's attempt to avoid physical confrontation. He was the instigator, the aggressor, the large man so unpredictable that he shouldn't be messed with.

"I was in Copley Mall one day," John says, referring to a popular shopping plaza in the heart of Boston. "My ex-girlfriend had a son. Great kid. I turned around to talk to somebody, and this guy was down on one knee and touching his face and talking to him. So, I see this and I smacked the guy. The guy gets up, and it turns out he's French. At first I was like, 'What the fuck are you talking to the kid for?' And then I thought, maybe in his country it's normal. Thank God I showed some self-control."

The kind, unsuspecting Frenchman who may have overstepped acceptable boundaries ran away licking his wounds. He had no interest in discovering what John was capable of doing next. Impulsivity is a weapon when wielded by men of violent predilections. It even instilled fear in John's gang friends. David Yee attempts to explain it this way: "He's an outsider. No matter how you play it, he's a white guy in an Asian world. His mystery put people on edge, but in reality, I think he was much more trustworthy than a lot of people I hung out with."

Still, being more trustworthy than most drug dealers and gang members is a relatively low bar, and when John drinks alcohol, even he acknowledges he can't be trusted. It seems to be a family thing.

"I believe everybody has inner demons," John begins. "When I'm drinking, I might get a chip on my shoulder about things that I've been through, and I might act on it. If I were not drinking, I would take the time to think about it. It scares me a lot when I drink, because I can't control what's happening. I'm sure a lot of it has to do with my father."

John's cousin Debbie agrees and offers additional perspective. "Let me tell you about the Willises," Debbie says. "Don't ever give us liquor. That goes for all the Willises. We've always had a temper. Living in the city like we did, you've got to be tough to survive. Dorchester is a tough town. It's not for the weak. Once John's anger kicked in, he would fly off the handle. He'd kick the shit out of someone. He didn't care. He didn't care if he got arrested."

And therein lies the danger. It's true John didn't care if he went to prison. He didn't care if he got into a fight with strangers or gangsters. He didn't fear the gun battles, and he was unconcerned about consequences. Now, whether it was apathy or an appalling arrogance that allowed John to behave as he did, he always acted with a presumed impunity, and it's part of what made him so scary.

"My heart was racing one night," David Yee recalls. "We were at a karaoke night at Wy Lu's in Saugus. We were all there. Ay-yat, Woping Joe, White Boy John. We were drinking. Talking about stupid shit. Nothing too personal, but John got pissed at Woping Joe. Suddenly, he looks at me and says, 'What the fuck are you going to do?' I was thinking of breaking a bottle and sticking him in the neck. He was carrying, and I wasn't. He's a big guy. I had to make sure he goes down fast."

It was an interesting group of friends out on the town just looking for a good time. First, there was Ay-yat, whom one Toronto investigator referred to as "the most dangerous Vietnamese gang-banger in North America." Next, there was David Yee, a loyal follower of Ay-yat since he was a teenager. Then there was Woping Joe, who was essentially born into the gang life, and White Boy John. Four tough guys. Four guys with a touch of crazy and great potential for violence. And the others looked at John as the toughest and craziest.

"There were plenty of times with John when I hung out with him and my friends, and I didn't know if we were cool," Yee admits. "I didn't know if this guy's going to pull a gun on me."

Yee says he had a "love and hate relationship" with John. Their connection began when John mediated a volatile issue between Yee and some gang kids. The relationship grew into a partnership as they worked on drug deals together, but it would be inaccurate to say it ever developed into a true friendship, because Yee admits he couldn't "one hundred percent trust that guy," adding, "When I was a rookie, I trusted everyone amongst me. Then you slowly see everything play out, and you realize you can't trust anyone."

The wall of distrust between Yee and John started to come down when they served time in jail together. In 1996, John was finally caught selling drugs and sentenced to six to eight years. He served a little over five years in the Massachusetts Correctional Institutions in Concord and Shirley.

"He was content in jail," Yee contends. "He wasn't weak at all. He was definitely strong, but he definitely had a lot of thoughts inside him. If this is it, he wondered if he could go through this anymore. We opened up to each other."

John and Yee weren't cellmates, but they spent a lot of time together in the yard during recreation time. Yee was imprisoned for participating in an armed home invasion when he was twenty-two years old. He and three other young Asian gang members had decided to rob the Quincy home of a local restaurant owner. Yee posed as a flower deliveryman. He rang the bell, and when a fifteen-year-old boy answered, Yee stuck a gun in his face and told him to get on the floor. Yee held the gun on the boy and repeatedly threatened to kill him while the other crooks ransacked the house. Yee and his cohorts tied the boy up with a telephone cord and left with several thousand dollars in cash, stereo equipment, and jewelry.

It took the boy only a few minutes to escape from his restraints and call the police. He identified the car as a late-model Nissan that was almost immediately spotted speeding through Quincy center. Sirens blared and the chase was on! Five minutes later the chase was over. The Nissan had crashed into a police cruiser. Yee was charged with home invasion, larceny, and assault and battery with a dangerous weapon. The police also searched the Nissan and discovered a 9mm handgun that had been stolen from a Shrewsbury gun shop seven years earlier. In 1996, Yee was sentenced to seven years, much of which he served with his associate White Boy John. He got to know John well enough to make several observations.

"I think that with everything considered," Yee says, "on the outside, I didn't trust him one hundred percent. But after the fact, after jail, I look back and I think I actually do trust this guy. My perspective when I was doing things with him was different. And he wants that trust so much. He thinks he's earned it. It's like, 'Don't question me.' He trusted Asian people at that time more than white people, but it slowly changed. First, trust was key with Asian people, but the people he trusted were turning more Americanized, and thinking about themselves. In essence, he was more Asian than the Asian guys. Was there some kind of loneliness after that? Totally. It's not a hundred percent what he really felt in his heart, but I know I pick up the loneliness."

It may be that John felt the alienation and despondency Yee refers to, but John also found peace in his jail-time solitude. As a free man, his days were nonstop business. He was always working on a deal, double-checking a delivery, and putting out fires. Inside the walls of a prison, he could relax. As they say, when you're doing time, you've got plenty of time. So, when John wasn't interacting with other inmates in the yard, at a poker table, or lifting weights, he went to the library and sat quietly reading books on Buddhism, tai chi, and other philosophies, and he took a particular liking to the Bible.

"The Bible is a book of rules," John explains. "I've been through it a hundred times. The first time was when I asked a guard for something to read, and he brought me the Bible. I was like, 'Okay, God, what are you saying to me right now? Am I supposed to read something in here? Should I find something in here to help comfort me?' So, I looked for something."

John opened the book somewhere near the middle, and flipped the pages forward and back before settling on the book of Job. He quickly found a kinship with Job, who had great wealth and a large family, but because of a random contest between God and Satan, Job lost everything. John thought about his early childhood when he felt rich riding his new bike or wearing his new sneakers, and he remembered some happier times when his mother was well, and before his brother and sisters were on drugs. He could relate to Job's situation and Job's internal dialogue.

The book of Job raises many questions about the relationship between God and man, and among the potential lessons it presents is the idea that God does not only punish the guilty. Innocent people like Job, who is described as "blameless and upright," are also made to suffer. Now, even though John also sees himself as blameless, he does not consider his earthly suffering as any kind of punishment for wrongdoing.

"Life is nothing more than a big game of lefts and rights," John theorizes. "It's how you take them, and what you do with it. People will say, 'I don't belong here. I don't deserve this.' And I'll stop them right in the middle of the sentence and say, 'This is exactly what you deserve.' Because your life is all about challenges, and what you do with them. Learn from what's put in front of you. I'll tell you the truth, this sucks being in prison. But I'll tell you what, there are trees in this compound and there are no towers with guys with machine guns, and I'm not getting shot at with rubber bullets. That could happen down the line. Who knows? Right now, I'm thankful. Whatever you learn, whatever you go through—that's exactly what you're supposed to go through. The guy who woke up with cancer one day, he didn't say, 'Oh, this wasn't supposed to happen.' He might think that, but this is what's supposed to happen. There's no bad luck. These are all predetermined destinations in our life through God."

As always, John remains a surprising source for a sermon, in large measure because he infuses his message of God with intimidation, intended or otherwise. He's so big, and his past so filled with violence, that the listener is left wondering whether he's being given an opinion or being ordered how to think. John's eyes are filled with a confusing intensity that is confirmed and compounded by the soft but forceful tone of his voice. He has a habit of sounding like a man desperately trying to hold back the forces of a violent outburst. He moves effortlessly between topics of God and love to casual recollections of murder and unintended outcomes.

"Gangsters are gangsters," John stipulates. "I don't see a problem with gangsters fighting gangsters. We're watching gambling houses, so if people come in to rob—we're there. We're also watching the people on the street, and taking care of the old ladies to make sure nobody messes with them. When we were kids, we stayed in Chinatown. We watched Chinatown. Now there's things like Neighborhood Watch. Neighborhood Watch is doing nothing more than telling the police after the crime has happened. When we were on the streets as children, you know, say sixteen, seventeen, eighteen years old, these people could walk around with red cellophane bags with fifty thousand, a hundred thousand dollars in it. Nobody's stopping them. Nobody's bothering them.

"Now there's, you know, rapes going on. There's people getting beaten up for money. There's old ladies getting robbed for pocketbooks. Why? Because now they've turned to the police instead of turning to the people who took care of Chinatown, made Chinatown different from everywhere else. Some people don't look at it that way, you know? You shoot an innocent lady coming out of church, then you're a hunk of shit. But that stuff doesn't happen. You don't ever hear about innocent people getting hurt in Chinatown. Just that one time with the girl from Medford."

Although John massively underestimates the number of non-gangsters being hurt in Chinatown, that "one time" he refers to is when an eighteen-year-old girl was used as a human shield during a gang-related shooting. Her name was Ky Ung Shin. She was a lovely young Korean girl, a volunteer at her church, and a junior at Medford High School. In the early evening of April 16, 1996, she was sitting at a table with two Asian friends at the Rainbow Restaurant in Chinatown. An argument erupted between her friends and three Asian males at another table. When the shooting started, one of Ky's friends pulled her in front of himself for protection. She was shot through the heart and died almost instantly. The two men she was with were both shot, but survived. The three other men ran out of the restaurant and down Oxford Street. All of the men, the shooters and the victims, were members of criminal gangs in Chinatown.

"There was a fight a couple of days before that," John explains. "And the guy came in to shoot. What happened was, about four days before, one of the younger kids from another faction jumped on my boss's brother's back. So, obviously something had to be done. So, the kid was sitting in the restaurant, and another kid walked in and just started shooting. The girl had just met these guys at a nightclub, and they asked her to come and hang out with them. Well, one of the guys grabbed the girl and pulled her in front of him. She got killed. He got hit in the thigh, and another kid got hit as well. The shooter is doing life. We called him Yen Do Jai, which means 'Indian boy.' The intended target was someone I'd rather not name."

The intended target was either Tran Phuoc Nguyen or Rick Lee. Those were the two men with whom the gunman had argued, and they were also the men who were treated for gunshot wounds to the groin and jaw, respectively. The shooter, a seventeen-year-old kid from East Boston, was captured three months later outside a mall in Warren, Michigan. John and David Yee talked about the shooting at lunch one day while serving time together in prison.

"You don't get points for hurting innocent people no matter how you look at it. You know what I mean?" John asked, but didn't wait for a response. "Women, children. I've seen it happen."

John didn't expound, nor did he mention the time their mutual friend Ay-yat shot up an entire coffee shop in Toronto just to get one person, although he didn't have to. David was already thinking about it, and John sensed it.

"That was crazy!" John said with a broad grin. "You know what I mean? But that's the way some people do things. When I was younger, sometimes it had to be done, you know, breaking legs and stuff. Shootings and stabbings. I'm not proud of those things. I don't have regrets for anything. The way I put it, there are two options in this life. We're sitting in one of them. The other is death."

John grinned broadly and gave David a nudge with his elbow as if to say, "Things could be worse." David forced an awkward smile, but he was clearly not in the mood to reminisce about the good old days or to look at the bright side of prison life. Soon after his jail cell door slammed shut for the first time, David was ready to go straight. The only thing he liked less than his life on the outside was his life on the inside. He was determined to get out and stay out. He talked with John about options and career opportunities, and even kicked around the idea of becoming an actor. The cage his body was in had freed his mind to imagine, to dream, and to write. David was discovering he had some talent.

"Well, I believe everything happens for a reason in life," John told him. "But I also believe you take a left or a right turn, or you just go straight ahead. So, it's all in the path we choose to walk, too."

David agreed and John continued.

"Principles," he said. "Always have principles. Never change your principles or your character for people. When you change, that's when you realize you made a mistake, because you're not supposed to change who you are. How many people do you see get into something—say, a bad acting job—people who are trying too hard to be somebody they're not? Same thing in life. This is me. This is who I am, you know. People might say to me, 'Are you remorseful?'

What am I remorseful for? This is what I do. This is who I am. I'm respecting the people who took care of me. So, I see nothing wrong with that."

David nodded, but he didn't actually agree. It was easier to feign concurrence than to tell John what he really thought—that people change all the time. He could have reminded his prison buddy that John wasn't always a gang criminal. He knew John was once a young boy devoted to caring for his sick mother. He was a good teammate on several youth hockey teams. He was a bright student with a bright future. But he changed when his mother died. The anger inside him calcified, and he grew to be apathetic about violence and consequences. This gangster John had become didn't have to be who he was or who he always would be. David considered telling John that he could change again. He could leave prison one day and become someone else. But when John talked about having no remorse, David knew John had no chance of truly changing. David and John had lived similar lives and had done similar things, but as they sat in prison together, there was one distinction of character that made them vastly different people: David felt remorse.

When he left prison, David got as far away from Massachusetts as he could. He moved to California and tried to make it as an actor and a screenwriter. He was able to change, if not himself then his path, and he successfully put his gang life behind him. John Willis, however, was unable or unwilling to change who he was. When he got out of prison, John found more trouble. He also found love.

SEVEN

JOHN WILLIS was in and out of prison several times for both short stints and lengthy stays between 1996 and 2008. Each arrest and conviction was a mere inconvenience and interruption of his thoroughly enjoyable life on the outside, which included selling drugs, driving fast cars, and chasing loose women. And there was plenty of each to go around.

Large-scale drug deals brought in large-scale profits, which led to the purchase of many expensive cars, motorcycles, and boats. Those material goods combined with John's big muscles, square jaw, steely eyes, and raging confidence led to many voluntarily sleepless nights with women who spent most of their days spinning around a pole.

John's nickname was "Captain Save-a-ho." It referred to his penchant for taking strippers off the stage, buying everything for them from cars and jewelry to furniture and groceries, and keeping a sexually gratifying relationship going until he lost interest. He was a player. And he had a lot of success finding the right kind of woman who was looking for the wrong kind of man. Then he met Anh Nguyen.

"It's just his personality," she begins. "You can tell he's an asshole, and I hear a lot of things people say about him, but to me, it's like he's a totally different person. He wasn't an asshole to me. He's always been very lovable and caring, and he's very attentive. It's totally opposite of what people say. Obviously, I do see that side of him with certain people, but he's always done right by me."

Anh is an exceptionally attractive Vietnamese woman, not petite, but tall and strong and statuesque. She appears physically hardened by hours in a gym, emotionally hardened by tragedy, and intellectually hardened by an understanding that her reality is one she's chosen. She could have had any man she wanted, but she willingly entered a relationship with a violent criminal, and she unabashedly acknowledges the inherent benefits and disadvantages of that choice. There was money. There was fun. There was love. And there was a nagging paranoia that a police investigation or a drug dealer's bullet could bring everything crashing down in an instant.

"I was not naive about where the money was coming from," Anh admits. In fact, she knew enough about John from the very beginning to realize the relationship was rife with pitfalls and likely doomed to fail, but she forged ahead anyway. That decision is as inexplicable as love.

"People warned me about the type of person he is," Anh explains. "First thing they will say is he's a player. He has money, and he will just play with you. They tell me he sells drugs and that he's a very violent person. But when John and I are together, he's a very different person. John is very genuine when he talks with me. Somewhere in my heart, I can see the way he looks at me, and the way he speaks to me. I feel like I can trust him."

Anh was born in Hanoi, Vietnam, on May 1, 1985. By age nine, she was sent to New York to live with a close family friend she calls Aunt Thu. Her parents divorced shortly thereafter, and Anh hasn't seen her father since. Her mother remarried, moved to the United States, and lives just a short distance away from Anh, but they do not speak to one another.

"I want no part of her," Anh says flatly. "I felt abandoned. I found love elsewhere. My aunt took great care of me."

Aunt Thu had family in Texas and moved Anh there to open a nail salon business when Anh was a teenager. Anh was an excellent student and remained so even after she became pregnant as a high school student. She kept her pregnancy a secret for the better part of five months before Aunt Thu noticed the belly bump.

"I was looking for love from somebody," Anh explains. "I found her father. His name is Luis. He's Mexican. I could relate to him. I thought it was love, and I found the attention that I needed. I didn't have the best support system.

But I knew the baby was a part of me and I wanted to keep her. There was no discussion with my aunt. I was raised in a strict Catholic family, so abortion wasn't allowed. Luis was very supportive. He wanted the baby. I wanted the baby even though I was still young."

My Linh was born on May 24 of Anh's sophomore year. Anh was sixteen years old when the doctor placed a beautiful baby girl in her arms, and she had no idea what to do. So, plans were made for her, and Anh went along, unwillingly at first.

"You're so brutal," Anh complained to her godmother, Hong. "I can't believe you make me do this!"

When My Linh was only a month old, Anh took her to Vietnam and left her with Hong.

"You hate me now, but you'll thank me someday," Hong said soothingly. "You want to go back with My Linh? Then you get married. I'll do all the arrangement for you. I'll let you go back if you agree to be married. Is that the life you want to live? You don't even have an education."

Anh realized marrying Luis wasn't the best thing for her own future or for My Linh's. She needed a good man, a steady man. Someone who would stay out of trouble. As difficult as it was, especially with the memory of her own parents sending her away, Anh decided to leave My Linh in Vietnam and return to finish high school in Texas.

"When I brought her back to Vietnam, I was on the plane by myself," Anh recalls. "I was crying. I refused to put her in the little bassinette. I carried her for the whole twenty-three hours. When I gave my godmother My Linh, my arms were so sore and tender from holding her. I couldn't feel my arms for a week. But as soon as I gave My Linh to my godmother, I knew she was in good hands. I slept for three days, you know, like a teenager."

Anh remained in Vietnam for My Linh's first summer, and then made the heartbreaking return trip to Texas, leaving My Linh behind. Anh cried inconsolably on the way to the airport, at the airport, and as she boarded the plane. Holding My Linh tightly, she wept tears of sorrow, guilt, and fear.

Stoically, Hong put one hand on Anh's shoulder and whispered: "Give it time. It heals everything."

Anh never did return to school in Texas. Instead, she was sent away again, this time to live with Thu's sisters in Massachusetts. She remained an excellent student and graduated from New Mission High School in Hyde Park, and immediately enrolled at the University of Massachusetts in Boston. She was a college sophomore and the mother of a four-year-old daughter thousands of miles away when she met John Willis in June of 2005.

"The night I met John," Anh begins, "they locked the club down. I heard somebody had a gun, and there was going to be a shootout."

It was at a bar called The 180 on Lincoln Street in Chinatown. Anh was twenty. John was thirty-four and in what for him would be considered a serious relationship, but that didn't slow him down. He spotted Anh and three of her girlfriends having trouble getting into the nightclub, which was already beyond capacity. They pleaded their case but were denied entry. So, they decided to leave and go to another nightclub. As they turned to walk away, John rushed up beside Anh and grabbed her hand.

"I just want to tell you you're drop-dead gorgeous," John blurted.

"What are you," Anh responded, "another one of these white boys with an Asian fetish?"

"No, I just think you're stunning," John said honestly, and then he turned to the bouncer, and barked, "Let her and her friends in."

As smitten as he was, John found himself being pulled in different directions throughout the course of the evening. He was unable to spend any quality time with Anh because everybody else wanted a piece of him, or some of his time. John was like a rock star in Chinatown, and he didn't mind showing that off to his latest pursuit, but Anh didn't take notice. She could tell John was much older than she was, and she wasn't initially attracted to him. So, she lost track of him and spent the night drinking and laughing with her friends. Late in the evening, word spread throughout the club that trouble was about to erupt between two guys with guns having a heated exchange. Patrons were rushing toward the exits when Anh overheard a man making threats in Chinese. When she turned around to see who it was, she was surprised to see the white guy who had gotten her into the bar.

"Oh, my God!" she exclaimed with great surprise. "You speak Chinese!"

"Of course I do," John said with a high degree of arrogance. "Why wouldn't I?"

Still unimpressed, Anh started to leave with her friends when John again grabbed her by the hand. This time he demanded her phone number.

"I don't give my number out to strangers," Anh protested.

"Well, if you don't give me your number," John explained flatly, "I'll be on your front step in the morning."

Anh hesitated as a series of important questions raced through her slightly drunken mind. Who was this guy, and how would he find out where she lived? Was he going to follow her home? Was his promise to be on her front step simply a flirtatious suggestion of persistence or an outright threat?

"Oh, give him your number," one of Anh's friends encouraged. "Maybe he can get us into another club sometime."

Anh relented and gave John her phone number. He called the next day, and they began what, for John, was a frustratingly and unusually long courtship.

"I tortured him for at least six months," Anh says with a laugh. "I remember there was a time I got locked out of the house, and John came over and said he would take me to a hotel. So, we laid on the bed together with all our clothes on, and I was like, 'Do not touch me!'"

John obeyed. He knew from the beginning he wanted something more, something different from Anh. The physical attraction was obvious, and he'd felt that before with hundreds of women, but Anh triggered something else inside him. She was smarter, stronger, and sassier than all of the women he'd been with. She was also unimpressed by his wealth and unintimidated by his power. John wasn't used to that, and he hadn't known any woman other than his mother who was as capably and resolutely independent as Anh. He loved her almost from the start, and if he could get her to love him, it would confirm for him what he always suspected was true: that he is a good man trapped inside a bad world.

And so he waited until Anh was ready. And while he waited, he lied to her and slept with other women. The lies and the unexpected guilt that came with them were simply evidence of love.

"Listen," John explains, "the other women served a purpose. We're men. We're not supposed to fuck around, but it happens. As men, we'll lie more to our wives than anyone else, because we really care what they feel. We won't lie to a guy in the street, because we don't give a fuck what he thinks."

Anh proceeded with caution into her relationship with John, in part because of his reputation, but primarily because of the fourteen-year age difference. She was more concerned about that than she was about John being a criminal. It seems as though the best thing that could have happened for John was surviving those first six months of "torture" that Anh put him through, because it was during that time that their bond was forged. Talking instead of having sex gave John a chance to explain who he is, or who he thinks he is, and why he is that way, and the devilishly good communicator was able to sell himself as loving, caring, and devoted. During the courtship, he lied to Anh, and he told her the truth. He opened up to her, and he shut her out. To her credit, Anh was able to discern the difference. Ultimately, she discovered the best parts of John and chose to overlook the rest.

"John and I share a lot in common," Anh reasons. "We're two different people. We're very different. I'm very calm. John can go from zero to a thousand in a split second. But as different as we are, we share the same values. I have a great support system, especially compared to John. I've never been homeless. My mom wasn't around, but I wasn't abandoned. I always had someone to take care of me. It wasn't easy, but compared to John, he didn't have any of that. But at the same time, I didn't have that motherly love or that fatherly love, and John didn't have that also. Since the day I met him, he never disappeared from my life. He has always been there for me. I've been there for him through a lot."

She stayed with John when he went to jail early in their relationship. She didn't run when she saw the drugs he was selling or the gun he was carrying. And she continued the relationship long after her suspicions of his violent nature were confirmed by witnessing it firsthand. The first time she saw blood on John's shirt and bruises on his knuckles, she asked him what had happened.

"Ah, some kid mouthed off," John replied.

The picture was coming more clearly into focus. The next time she saw blood on John's shirt, she knew exactly how it got there, because she watched him beat a man unconscious. The victim was a drunken fool who stumbled into Anh at a nightclub, causing her to drop the flowers John had given her. Too drunk to notice what he had done, or that he had also stepped on the flowers, the drunken man compounded the sin by not apologizing.

"John beat the shit out of the guy," Anh recalls.

The furious rage and power that John exudes when he's beating someone is a big part of why his enemies feared him and even his closest friends were cautious around him. Nobody knew what would cause him to snap—only that when he did, his brute force would be merciless.

"John, stop!" Anh screamed, as the man lay motionless on the floor. She put her arm on John's shoulder to pull him off the man, and when John turned around she saw the demon look in his eyes for the first time. He was about to take a swing at whoever was tugging at him, but when he realized it was Anh, the beast was soothed.

"What the hell was that for?" Anh demanded to know as others went to the aid of the pulverized man.

"He was being fucking disrespectful," John defended himself. "Not only did he knock the flowers out of your hand, but he also stepped on them. He should have fucking apologized! I did that for you."

"It was an accident," Anh argued.

But John didn't see it that way. He sees it this way: "Sometimes people don't know the right thing until you beat it into them," he says. "Sometimes you need to hurt people to make them understand. Explaining it to them won't get it done."

Anh swears she's never been fearful of John, not even in that moment when she was trying to restrain him and she caught a glimpse of his internal rage. She acknowledges they've had their share of heated arguments, and that she's thrown a coffee mug or two at him, but she says he's never hit her or grabbed her or even threatened to hurt her. Not every woman in John's past can say the same.

"I've made mistakes in my life where I've disrespected women and I felt horrible about it later," John explains. "I hate that feeling. I feel like a nickel. It just makes me feel terrible. There are times when I've called Anh a 'c-word.' Now in those cases, I called her a name that I definitely don't mean. I disrespected her. I got nowhere with it. And I'm wrong at the end of all this. I wasted time, made myself look bad, and I'm still wrong. That sums it up for me."

"When he snaps," Anh continues, "it's because he has a lot of anger inside him, but also that's all he knew growing up, from the people he surrounded himself with and how they dealt with things. I've seen the demon side of him come out with everybody else, but not with me. John loves everyone, unless you cross him. It doesn't take much to get on his bad side. He has so much pride. As soon as he feels disrespected, he will put you in your place. He really lives by principle."

Anh is well rehearsed in the art of defending John. She's been engaging in it from the very beginning. She had to defend him to her girlfriends, who openly questioned whether it was a good idea to date an unreformed and unrepentant criminal. She had to explain to her aunts that John was really a good man deep down, and that he always treated her well. Even in her own mind, she had to make numerous rationalizations, concessions, and compromises to convince herself that being with John was the best thing for her future.

When Anh first met John, she was enrolled at the University of Massachusetts in Boston, and she eventually transferred to Quincy Community College. She was a business major with an eye on helping her aunts run a nail salon in East Boston. She was honest and responsible, and she had goals. Her plan was to finish her education and then bring her daughter, My Linh, back from Vietnam. Those plans changed after she became involved with John. First, she cut back on her college course load, and then she ultimately quit school just a few credits shy of her degree. Finally, she acquiesced to John's incessant pleading that she bring My Linh home.

"When Anh and I started dating," John explains, "I said, 'You should bring My Linh home. What's she doing over there? You go get her, and I'll help take care of her.' That was my biggest goal—to make sure everything was good for her."

Anh wasn't initially ready to share her daughter with the absentee father and criminal she'd just met, but after they'd been dating for about two years, John and Anh moved in together, and Anh went to Vietnam and returned with My Linh. Finally, John had a family!

"I screwed up my life," John admits, "but I look at My Linh, and I won't screw up hers. Anh's been through a lot in her life. Hard life. And then to stick with me when I'm a boy instead of a man. When you're out on the street, you're playing. We do as we do as men, especially in my life. Money, women, there's all kinds of crazy shit that goes on. No set of everyday rules. No waking up at 8 A.M. to go to work. It's different. She brought me to a point where the need to be with her was so great that I would change my ways of doing things. I looked at people and I never looked at things from their side. She taught me to have some kind of compassion for other people. Especially with My Linh. Her biggest thing was, 'Are you going to take care of My Linh?' And that was the biggest promise of my life. I couldn't fulfill that for my own sons. I wasn't ready to be a dad, but I felt like I had to with My Linh. I'll never walk away from her."

It remains a challenging pursuit to match the person John thinks he is with the actions that reveal someone quite different. He talks about having compassion, but he sets it aside whenever it suits him. He says he'd never abandon My Linh, but circumstances he brought on himself have caused him to do just that. And he claims his love for Anh changed him in significant ways, but the changes he genuinely believes he made are imperceptible to others.

For instance, the compassion he found for others didn't prevent him from hitting a parking lot attendant with the butt end of a gun. He was with Anh and My Linh. The newly formed family was going out to dinner in Chinatown. John parked where he always parked, but the new attendant didn't know John or the special arrangement he had with the owner of the lot. The attendant started yelling at John to move his car. So, John sent Anh and My Linh into the restaurant. Once they were out of view, he joined the attendant inside the glass booth and closed the door behind him.

"Hey, fuck you!" the attendant shouted. "You can't be in here."

"Do you know me?" John asked in a calm, low voice.

"Fuck you," the attendant said again. So, John showed him his gun and then clubbed him with it above the left eye.

"My name is John. Ask around. People will tell you who I am. And don't disrespect me ever again."

John left the attendant bleeding inside the booth, and joined Anh and My Linh for dinner. John was relaxed and in a good mood while he ate. He sat there as if nothing had happened, and in truth, nothing out of the ordinary had happened. John dealt with a minor indiscretion with his garden-variety intimidation. The attendant had stepped out of line and needed to be taught a lesson through both pain and fear. For John, the situation was handled properly and now the matter was closed. So, he ate a hearty meal, left a big tip, and returned to his car. Obviously, someone had explained John's status in Chinatown to the attendant, because he was standing by John's car when John came out of the restaurant. Anh noticed the golf ball–sized welt on the attendant's forehead, and she looked disapprovingly at John.

"You said you didn't do anything," Anh rebuked, as she got into the car and slammed the door. John just shrugged.

"I'm so sorry," the attendant began. "I didn't know. I will quit my job tomorrow. Please forgive me!"

"Don't quit," John said. "It's all over now."

"I must quit," the man insisted. "I have done wrong. I'm only here now to make things right with you and to wait for my daughter."

"You have a daughter?" John asked, and upon hearing that Anh put the window down in the car and told John to apologize to the attendant.

"I'm not going to apologize," John protested. "He was wrong."

"You hit him," Anh explained as if to a child. "Apologize to him, and don't let him quit his job."

To keep the peace at home, John did as he was told, but the attendant remained insistent that he should quit. At first,

John tried begging him not to quit, and when that didn't work, he pulled the attendant aside and resorted to the only sure thing.

"If you quit your job," John said very softly, "I will beat the living shit out of you."

The attendant was back to work the next day, and John was left with a story that he tells as proof that he is willing and able to change for Anh, and that because of her, he showed the attendant uncustomary compassion. The original violence and the threat of more violence notwithstanding, John claims he saw the attendant as a person, and as a father who needed a job to support his daughter. He felt sympathy and showed mercy, and neither was likely to occur before he met Anh.

"It changes you as a person," John persists. "Anh really made me a better person. Let's be honest, I've never met a better person than her. She sees the good in everybody."

Still, his love for her did not persuade him to remain faithful to her. For the first two years of their relationship, John was seeing another woman. Anh found out when the mistress called her up and told her. This other woman was hoping that Anh would be so irate that she'd leave John. Instead, Anh told the mistress, "I'm glad he was nice to you, but he's not going anywhere. We have a daughter together, and our bond will never change."

That was the moment that Anh threw herself completely into her relationship with John. Had she learned of his infidelity before My Linh came to live with them, she might have walked away. She certainly doesn't seem like the kind of woman who would tolerate cheating.

"I didn't think I would, either," Anh explains. "But I guess when I was put in that position, and we were together for a while, I guess if you love someone, you accept it, and you let it go. I thought about leaving him, but you can't pick and choose who you love, right? Sometimes it's hard. And I just felt like what John and I shared even through his stupidity and all that, I just felt like we do have a kind of bond I don't see in other people, you know."

It was, however, a strange declaration to say they had a daughter together, considering that My Linh had only met John a few months earlier. But in that short time, Anh saw what she needed to see. John and My Linh made an instant connection, and John was ready to be a father.

"I think what attracts me more to him than anything was the way he was with my daughter," Anh says. "It takes a real man to raise another man's child, and be really close to her. Sometimes I think the reason he's so passionate about kids is because, first of all, John has kids of his own, but he wasn't able to be a part of their lives. He lost out on the chance of being a father. He feels badly about that. But when he feels badly, he moves on. My Linh gave him a second chance at being a father."

John loved having a daughter. The day My Linh arrived, he took his new precocious four-year-old into Chinatown. At the bakery, My Linh pushed her way to the front of the line and pointed at the cakes and pastries behind the glass. John bought her whatever she wanted. Next, he took her to the gambling houses as if it were "take your daughter to work day." Inside the rooms filled with gamblers and smoke, My

Linh was treated like a princess. And why not? John was the king of Chinatown.

"My Linh, to me, why she's so important, because she's my daughter," John explains. "That's the way I look at it. No matter what happens, she's my daughter. I'm going to take care of her. If somebody hurts one hair on her head I'm gonna do whatever I gotta do to make them feel the same pain. You may say, 'Why do you liken it to violence or pain?' Well, it's about protection. To protect your family sometimes you gotta be that person, because people will take you to the limit. That's what this world is about. Everybody wants to push the limit. Everyone. Even the people who run the government. They'll take a little at a time. They'll take more next year. Everybody pushes until you step up and say, 'Don't push.' So, with My Lynn, I don't play games. I cut right to the chase. That's my little girl."

Unfortunately, a few months after meeting his little girl, John went back to prison. He sold marijuana to a few guys he didn't know too well. When he went to a house in Dorchester to make the deal, the buyers showed John a duffel bag full of machine guns, and they asked if he wanted to buy them. John declined, but one of the buyers was actually an informant, and when he told his FBI handlers that John was there, the FBI knew they had John on a parole violation and used that fact to try to squeeze information out of him. John was at a pizza restaurant when he was arrested and brought to South Boston for questioning.

"We know you know about the guns," an FBI agent barked.

"Am I being charged with guns?" John asked.

"No."

"Then why are you talking to me about guns? I got nothing to say to you."

"We've got you on a parole violation," the agent asserted. "You're going back to prison. Don't you want to help yourself?"

"Help myself how? By helping you?" John replied. "No thanks. I got six months left. I'm going back to jail."

"Have it your way," a Boston cop said, leaning in close to John. "Just know that we're going to get you."

John gave it his best tough guy smile, but he knew he had a couple of powerful enemies, cops who were ready to make it their life's mission to bring him down. He returned to state prison in Concord, Massachusetts, and served out the rest of his time, which was actually eight more months. Anh spoke to him every day on the phone, but never visited, nor did John ever see My Linh for those eight months. The father figure she had grown close to was quickly and suddenly gone from her life.

"It's torture," John says of being away from Anh and My Linh. "It's not easy at times to be away from somebody you love more than anybody you've ever loved in your whole life. I've never loved another human being the way I love Anh, or My Linh. How much can you convey that when you're sitting in jail?"

If that were said with zealous conviction, you might expect the speaker to make every effort to never return to jail. John, however, came out of jail with a plan that he knew full well could send him right back—and for a very long time.

"We're not going to get into a little trouble," John told his new accomplices. "We're going to get into a lot of trouble. We're not about to do things on a small level. I'm not out to make a hundred thousand. I'm out to make a hundred million."

A lot of money was about to be made, but first John had a double funeral to attend.

EIGHT

"WHEN SHE LOOKS AT ME," John says about My Linh, "it stops my heart."

Although John has never officially adopted My Linh, he speaks as a proud father. He has assumed the role and the responsibility of a fully committed parent, and he has discovered the many conflicts inherent in loving and properly raising a child.

"I take parenting the way I take life," he says thoughtfully. "I evaluate the situation. I value people. I value My Linh. I know what's going to make her smile, and what's going to make her feel bad. I try to discipline her, but I also try to give her everything she wants. One time she got me mad, and I put her in her room with the light off. That hurt me more than it did her. I'll never do that again. As a parent, I want her to have nothing but good things. I don't think I'm a bad person or a bad parent."

Of course, the arrival of My Linh further domesticated John. He remained a drug-dealing enforcer who routinely carried a gun, but he also got up in the morning and made breakfast for a small child. He frequently took her to school, and picked her up in the afternoon. He took her ice skating for the first time, and played in the snow. He held her hand, kissed her round face, and loved to have her fall asleep on his chest. In those moments, John was at peace. There were no drug deals to be made, no battles to be won, and no cops harassing him. Perhaps an important part of John's childhood was lost when his brother died and he was forced to take care of his ailing mother. He was still a boy, but carrying the burdens of a man. Now, as a man standing in the doorway of My Linh's bedroom and watching her sleep, he often felt nostalgic for the lost innocence of his own youth.

"You can't dislike a child," John asserts. "Kids only know what we show them. A child is a product of their environment. You see a bad kid, don't look at the kid. Look at the parent. It's not the kid's fault. They don't know wrong unless they're taught wrong. They won't swear unless they hear it. Me—in Chinatown—I used to give them candy. But times have changed. Now parents look at you weird. A couple of times I'd snap at the parent, 'What the fuck are you looking at?' But I guess they're just looking out for their kid. I love children, because they're just innocent."

And while John has a fondness for innocence and simplicity, he had no interest in rediscovering either. Too much had happened in his life. He was far too entrenched in his criminal ways to be swayed in the direction of a traditional family life by the slight tug of an adorable child. Yes, he loved Anh and My Linh as much as he could, and he entertained a fleeting thought about trying to go straight, maybe opening a legitimate business, but a life of dinner at six and falling asleep in front of the television was not for John. His past criminal enterprises had left him with enough money to begin a new life, but he wanted more than enough money, and he liked his old life. He was good at that one. And he was determined to use the additions of Anh and My Linh to his life as motivation—not to change, but to improve: to go bigger!

"I've always wanted to give My Linh everything," John explains. "And that's been my drive to do everything. What's the point of having money if you don't take care of your family? I've never told Anh 'no' to anything. The reason we do this stuff is to have nice things and to live a good life."

So, when John got out of jail in 2008, he walked through the front door of his home and surprised Anh with flowers. Anh wasn't expecting him home that day, and while she was excited to see him, her joy was surpassed by a sudden sense of relief.

"Finally," she thought, "help has arrived."

It had been difficult for Anh to go from being a college student and party girl to a single mom almost overnight. When she first brought My Linh home from Vietnam, John was there to help, but he went off to prison in a matter of months. Anh could always count on her aunts Kimberly and Lilly to help, but Kimberly had a daughter of her own, and Lilly was finishing up school at Wesleyan University in Connecticut. So, as Anh welcomed John home with hugs and kisses and more, she thought about how nice it would be for John to get My Linh from school while she took a nap.

"The first thing I said to My Linh was I loved and missed her so much," John says. "From that point on, my relationship with My Linh was growing so strong! I took her everywhere with me. All the people in Chinatown treat her like a princess. She gets love everywhere she goes. And that makes me happy."

Soon after the tearful reunion and the bedtime stories were read to an attentive My Linh, John returned to the streets. He still had his connections and his reputation, so it wasn't difficult to come out of jail and hit the ground running.

"What does the street want?" John asked himself. "What's big now? At one point it was commercial marijuana. Then it went to the B.C. bud out of British Columbia and then it went to the high-end stuff out of California. So you change with the times. You roll with it."

John prided himself on outthinking, outworking, and, if need be, outmuscling everyone else in his line of business. He doggedly pursued the next deal, but when he was introduced to the next best thing, he was surprised and suspicious, and then he was quickly convinced.

"The idea came by total accident," John begins. "A kid came to me who owed me money. He told me about these pill mills in Florida. The street wants pills, you go and get some pills."

A pill mill, according to Pam Bondi, the attorney general of Florida, is an "unscrupulous" doctor's office, clinic, or health care facility "that merely serves as a drug trafficker. Common characteristics of pill mills include cash only/no insurance, no appointments, armed guards, few or no medical records, grossly inadequate physical examinations, and large prescription doses of narcotics that exceed the boundaries of acceptable medical care."

In 2009, a few months after John got out of jail, there were nine hundred registered pain management clinics in Florida. The primary drug these clinics prescribed was oxycodone, which is considered heroin in pill form and is sold under the brand name OxyContin. In 2010, ninety-eight of the top one hundred oxycodone-dispensing physicians in the nation were located in Florida. In those years, 89 percent of all the oxycodone sold in the United States was sold from those nine hundred pill mills in Florida, most of it from walk-in, cash-only, no-insurance-necessary clinics. That's where John needed to be.

"I told this guy it didn't sound right," John says of his initial skepticism, "but I went down to Florida to check it out. It just so happened that a friend of mine worked in these places, and he called me up and said it was a good deal. I said okay. After a month of doing it, I had a lot of money. It was crazy! I had a room filled with safes that each had $88,000 in it. I had more than twenty safes."

It took a while to amass that kind of money, but not a long while. John had inadvertently stepped into the underworld of dealing oxycodone. The Florida pain clinics had turned the state into the "Columbia of prescription drugs," and the pills were being dispensed by doctors best characterized as "drug dealers with degrees." In 2009 and 2010, there were more than twenty-seven thousand oxycodone fatalities in Florida, and many more deaths in Kentucky, Ohio, West Virginia, and Tennessee were traced back to Florida. John and his coconspirators were among the many who took advantage of Florida's deregulated prescription medicine laws. John had a couple of guys on the inside, and several other men and women engaging in what was known as "doctor shopping," in which they could go to many different doctors and get prescriptions for oxycodone from each. In a matter of weeks, the addicts or dealers were able to amass prescriptions for a year's worth of oxycodone. Willis and his gang were able to traffic hundreds of thousands of oxycodone pills from Florida up the East Coast all the way to Cape Cod, Massachusetts.

With his lion's share of the profits, John bought expensive cars and boats, as well as a $2.3 million home on the Intracoastal Waterway in Florida just outside Fort Lauderdale. He even attempted to go somewhat legit by giving his friend Brant Welty $70,000 to help purchase a liquor store in Massachusetts. John also cut a deal to buy a nightclub in Florida. He was in the process of opening that club in

November of 2010 when he and Anh erupted into a familiar argument.

"You've been in Florida for two weeks!" Anh shouted. "You just get home, and now you're leaving again?"

"I have to," John explained. "I'm not a business suit standing on the sidelines. I'm supposed to be there to do the paperwork."

"But I need you," Anh persisted. "And My Linh misses you."

"Don't do that," John said defensively. "I put her and you before everything. I know at times it doesn't seem like it, but it's true. Jesus, Anh! I'm opening a fucking nightclub! I can't be here and there at the same time."

The television happened to be on while they were arguing, and a breaking news alert came across the screen. John and Anh might not have noticed except that they distinctly heard the words "three dead in a Lynnfield shooting." The victims were not identified, but Anh was horrified and suddenly had a terrible, sickening feeling. Instinctively, she knew something tragic had happened to her cousin and her aunts.

"Don't be crazy," John said intuitively. "Lynnfield's a big place."

Anh frantically began calling her aunts Kimberly and Lilly, who lived in Lynnfield. She tried their home phone. There was no answer. She speed dialed each of their cell phones. Again, no answer. She even tried the cell phone of Kimberley's twelve-year-old daughter, Stephanie, but there was no answer there either. It was just after eleven o'clock at night on a Monday. Where was everyone?

John volunteered to take Anh to her aunts' home. He was hopeful it would provide comfort to Anh, but he, too, was alarmed when no one had answered her phone calls. They took My Linh to their downstairs neighbors, and raced to Lynnfield. John held Anh's hand the whole way while Anh shook nervously in the seat next to him. The blue flashing lights on a half dozen State Police cars outside Kimberly and Lilly Nguyen's house brought Anh's heart into her stomach. John, too, fought back tears, knowing that the worst had happened.

"First, we thought the little girl, Stephanie, was killed," John recalls. "But she was safe."

Stephanie was able to escape from the house unharmed. She ran next door, and while she quivered at the kitchen table, horrified neighbors called 911. They relayed what Stephanie had told them. Her mother, Kimberly Nguyen, and her aunt, Lilly Nguyen, had both been shot and killed by Kimberly's boyfriend, Joseph Cummings. Stephanie witnessed Lilly's murder, but closed her eyes when Cummings sat down next to her mother and turned the gun on himself. The details Stephanie has been able to express provide a chilling account of the chaotic episode.

Fifty-one-year-old Joseph Cummings had a long criminal history that included arrests for both violent and nonviolent crimes, and though he'd never been convicted of domestic violence, two prior girlfriends were successful in obtaining restraining orders against him. He had been dating Kimberly for about two years, and living with her nearly as long. Neighbors heard them arguing frequently, but it was nothing that they considered ominous. On the night of November 23, 2010, Kimberly and Joe had their last argument. It was about what to name their unborn child. Kimberly was six months pregnant.

As the argument escalated, Cummings went downstairs and retrieved two handguns. He was calm and deliberate in his movements, almost as if he were in a trance. His arms were at his sides with a gun in each hand as he slowly walked back up the stairs. Lilly, who had feared the worst and was spying from the top of the stairs, saw the guns and ran screaming down the hallway, pulling Stephanie into a back bedroom. Lilly shouted warnings to Kimberly, who remained in the master bedroom.

"Hide, Kimberly! He has a gun!"

There was no time to try to lock the door, so Kimberly sat on the bed and began praying and pleading for her life. Cummings was unmoved. Lilly and Stephanie heard the unmistakable sound of several shots being fired, and they both shrieked in horror knowing that Kimberly was dead.

Lilly was the first to be able to move. She ran to the window, opened it wide, and pleaded with Stephanie to jump out, but Stephanie was still too frightened to move.

"I'll jump first," Lilly said. "Then you jump and I'll catch you."

Stephanie nodded slightly, but as Lilly turned to jump, Cummings appeared in the doorway and fired one deadly accurate shot into her back. Lilly fell out the window and died in the bushes below.

That left Stephanie and Cummings alone in the bedroom. He was not her father, and he had never taken much of a liking to her. In his maniacal state anything was possible. Stephanie looked up at Cummings who stared her down unsympathetically. No words were spoken, and Stephanie braced for the worst. She closed her eyes and clenched her fists. Her entire body was rigid. She stood that way for what seemed like minutes, and then she was jolted by the sound of one final gunshot.

"He went back to the master bedroom, sat down right next to my aunt, and shot himself," Anh says sadly.

Kimberly Nguyen had come to the United States from Vietnam as a teenager. She pursued the American dream and opened her own business, the House of Nails, in East Boston. She was thirty-five years old when a sporadically employed carpenter shot her in the head several times.

Lilly Nguyen had earned a bachelor's degree from Wesleyan University in Connecticut and was applying to medical schools when she died in the bushes at the age of twenty-nine.

Stephanie Nguyen was physically unharmed in the tragic incident, but mentally traumatized.

"She's never gonna be the same, you know?" Anh says. "But she's a really strong person, and she's really smart, like ever since that happened with her mom, she has always kept high honor roll in school. Even with that, even under the pressure, she never missed a test."

On the night of the murders, John and Anh stood outside, bathed in flashing blue lights, knowing only that three people in the house were dead. They looked on helplessly. It was a dreadful several minutes before a police officer informed them that the victims included two adult females and one adult male.

"What about the girl?" Anh cried with both hope and despair. "Where's Stephanie?"

"She's safe," the officer said. "I'll take you to her."

John and Anh followed the officer, but when it became obvious he was leading them to the neighbor's house, Anh pulled away from John and ran swiftly past the officer. She swung open the front door, and called out Stephanie's name several times. Stephanie stood up from a kitchen chair and suddenly felt the strong bear hug of her cousin. Anh squeezed tightly and sobbed hysterically. Stephanie felt the love and the warmth and gradually stopped shivering, but tears continued to roll down her face.

"Why did he kill the baby?" she asked over and over.

John and Anh took Stephanie to her father's house. Tony Nguyen hadn't heard the news, and he cried when John told him what had happened. He was suddenly charged with raising a traumatized twelve-year-old girl alone. He accepted the responsibility and has done the best he can, though John still considers him a "snake." He's given him a beating more than once and welcomes any opportunity to do so again.

"Let's just say he's lucky he has a daughter," John threatens.

As Stephanie's father, and with no one else named to inherit Kimberly's nail salon, Tony fought for control of the business. According to John and Anh, he had no interest in actually running it, or any knowledge of how to, so he and Anh became partners.

"He wanted to take everything away from my family," Anh explains. "That's when John stepped in. He made him sign the paper. So, he and I are partners. I run the business. I'm the face of the business. Tony eats off me every two weeks, but the way I look at it, it's for Stephanie. I'm trying to retain what belonged to my aunt for her."

Stepping in to take care of the family business is one of the reasons Anh has never completed her college degree. Once again, her life had taken an unexpected and dramatic shift. And once again, she would deal with it with fearless resolve. She had done so when she became pregnant as a high school freshman, and again when she took My Linh to Vietnam, and later when she decided to raise My Linh on her own. There was also a fearless resolve in her relationship with John, especially when she considered the fate of her aunts at the hands of a man with a violent temper.

"After that happened to my aunts," Anh admits, "people would say to me, 'We always thought that was something that would happen to you.'"

Anh eventually grew tired of defending John to people who only knew him by reputation. She was content with the man she knew and loved, and she never feared for her own safety or My Linh's. Besides, she was too busy to concern herself with the concerns of others. She suddenly had a business to run, and she ran it well. With John's help, she got My Linh up and off to school in the mornings and made the short trip from their Dorchester home to East Boston, where she helped turn a nice profit at the House of Nails. With John's money nearly as her own, she didn't have to work as hard as she did, but she wanted to remain somewhat independent. Maybe she worried that John wouldn't always be around. He could be killed or sent to jail, and then what would she do? So, she worked.

"I work hard for my money," she says. "Even if there were a couple of hundred thousand dollars in the safe, I never ask John for a dollar. I would not ask him for any of it, unless it was something very expensive, and I want him to get it for me. I always had a job and I would buy things for myself. When I go shopping, I have my own money in my pocket, and I get what I want."

With Anh working full-time, much of the logistical child-rearing responsibilities fell to John. He did most of his illegal work at night, so his days were free to be a dad. He enjoyed picking up My Linh from school and taking her to various activities. While they drove, John helped My Linh with her English, and she learned quickly.

As they drove and talked and got to know each other, My Linh touched something in John he had never felt before. With Anh, he found true love for the first time, but with My Linh, he found vulnerability, even mortality. He wasn't afraid to die, but he had a new reason to live. He needed to be around for this precious little girl. He felt an immediate obligation to take care of her, to nurture her, and to teach her. There was so much she needed to know.

"I tell her, 'If somebody hits you, hit them back.' Telling on somebody is just passing the ball to somebody else—a teacher, whatever. People won't believe you half the time if you tell anyway. So, don't tell on them. Hit them."

John looked at the innocence and kindness of My Linh with wonder. He also couldn't help noticing how those qualities contrasted with his own inner demons. He recognized in a larger sense that there was room for both good and evil in the world, and while he never for an instant second-guessed the way he lived his life, he was confronted with a new curiosity. When love, in its various forms, entered his life, John's self-worth and self-identification were somewhat shaken. His love for Anh led him to crave her acceptance, but from My Linh, he needed respect, and he wasn't convinced she would see him as respectable if she knew his true self. After all, she was just a child. How could she possibly understand that God had offered him only one path, and that he had pleased God by making the most of his one opportunity?

He did his best to separate his two worlds. My Linh would know him as a legitimate businessman. He would pose as a typically domesticated father. Their lives would be normal. And in John's mind, his ability to create this new persona was not an act of self-abnegation. He was not motivated by humility or embarrassment. There was no acknowledgment of wrongdoing. He was merely broadening the definition of his true self. He was no longer just a gangster. He was a man in love who needed love in return, and who was capable of great kindness when it was called for.

"If I have to threaten you to do something," John often reasoned, "you made that happen. I don't want to be that person people want me to be."

It's as if he convinced himself that the violent criminal in him was a necessary part of himself dragged out of him by circumstances, and that the doting father he presented to My Linh was much more genuine. And to maintain that core belief, all he had to do was keep his two worlds, and his two personalities, separate.

"There was a time My Linh was on my lap," John begins. "And I don't know if she saw the gun or felt the gun when she leaned against me, and for a second I felt, I don't know, kind of like dirty. I felt bad. My wife said, 'I told you not to bring that around.' At that time, I said, 'You're right. I shouldn't have this around.' That put things into perspective for me. I shouldn't intermingle my two worlds."

But John did merge his two worlds in the most obvious and dangerous way possible. He flashed his money. Every criminal knows to keep a low profile and not to draw attention to himself, but John, who had no visible means of support, drove around in a Bentley Coupe. The police in the blue-collar communities of Dorchester and Chinatown noticed. The FBI noticed. The DEA noticed. It was an uncharacteristically dumb move.

"Life always offers choices," John explains. "You know where to go when you get to the fork in the road, but sometimes that wrong road looks pretty good. You see yourself driving a Bentley, or a million-dollar boat, but money has never ruled me. I always say it doesn't matter, because God loves me. I'm always going to make money and take care of my family. Money comes and goes. You can't possibly think if you're driving a Bentley that there's no repercussions. There are people who are jealous. People will see. Was it self-destructive? Let's just say I was very naive to the way the government works. I thought they had to catch you doing something. If you have a gun, that's a gun charge. Drugs, that's a drug charge. But driving around in a Bentley, what's the crime? Why would I be stopped and asked where I got it just because I didn't have a job?"

John always assumed he was being watched and that his phones were tapped, and he was very careful. He had five cell phones and spoke on them in a cryptic, coded Chinese. Anybody listening would have tremendous difficulty understanding what was being said or what it meant. He also paid people to do the transactions, so his hands were clean. It was a game he played every day, and he played it well.

"It's like chess," he says. "You know what you have to do. Always thinking two or three moves ahead. If you're making waves, it's going to be a rough swim. Make the peace with people you need to make peace with. And you try to stand on the tallest mountain of money at the end. You do what you have to do, and you get through it. Now, if somebody thinks I'm coming by to take his head off, when I show up, I better take his head off."

Perhaps the game was like chess, and if so, then it is equally true that John was arrogant enough to believe the rest of the world was playing checkers. Covering every angle and foreseeing every problem kept the risk low and the rewards high. In a matter of months of selling oxycodone, John had those safes full of cash. He had great wealth and the love of a good woman and precious child. He had everything, but he wanted everything else. He wanted more. And when he got more, it was never enough. Turns out, he wanted more than enough, and he'd get that, too.

"The money was easy to make," he boasts. "It's just human nature. When you make so much money, greed takes over you. When you're making a hundred thousand a week, how are you going to stop that?"

By getting caught.

NINE

JOHN WILLIS was fast becoming the man! He was the leader of a drug conspiracy that trafficked hundreds of thousands of oxycodone pills and generated more than $4 million in proceeds. He introduced several previously small-time criminals to great wealth at what seemed to be low risk. But in order to make as much money as possible, the inner circle needed to expand.

The conspiracy began when John met a man named Stanley Gonsalves while they were both in prison in 2009. Gonsalves was from Cape Cod, but he knew a guy, Peter Melendez, who worked security at an imaging center, a well-known pill mill in Florida. Melendez, nicknamed "Shrek" because of his cartoonish, ogrelike appearance, was arrested for marijuana possession in December of 2009. He was back on the streets in time to meet with John and Gonsalves and explain to them how the scheme worked. Melendez said his roommate, Brian Bowes, was also a security guard at another MRI clinic, and he should also be brought in on the deal.

"They became the brokers," John says. "They had connections in the business for so long."

This new drug business was up and running in a hurry. Bowes and Melendez had the connections in Florida, and the easy access to the pills. John and Gonsalves had the connections in Massachusetts where the pills could be distributed and sold.

"I get a lot of these pills and distribute them to two people," John explains. "After that, I'm done. I didn't sell drugs on the street. Never would. I didn't want to do that. I didn't have the time for that shit."

The business model was simple. The pills were gathered in Florida and flown by courier to Boston. The courier was typically a young female who was attractive, inconspicuous, and ideally, drug addicted. These women were willing to work for short cash, unlimited drugs, and the opportunity to dine in fancy restaurants, drive in nice cars, and sleep with men just coming into big money. One of those women was Nina O'Shay, a twenty-year-old drug addict who was handpicked by Gonsalves.

"He had just gotten out of jail," Nina would later testify. "He asked my friend, his cousin Karen, for my number. She said, 'Yeah, but you have to give me money, and I'll give you her number,' because it's just how she is. So, he gave her like three or four 30-milligram Percocets for my number, and he started texting me."

Nina and Gonsalves were sleeping together within a few weeks, and a few weeks after that, she unwittingly became his personal driver and a frequent flyer to and from Florida. The first time she laid eyes on John was at a car wash at the bottom of the Neponset River Bridge in Quincy, Massachusetts. A woman named Samantha Park drove Gonsalves up from Yarmouth on the Cape to meet John. Nina was in the backseat of their blue Hyundai Sonata, disinterested and reading a book. Sam parked the car next to John's maroon Hummer, and noticed John was driving and Pete Melendez was in the passenger seat. Sam and Gonsalves got out to talk with John and Pete. After about fifteen minutes, they returned to the car and drove back to the Cape. Nina didn't understand until much later that it had been decided at the car wash meeting that she would begin driving for Gonsalves and flying to and from Florida with drugs and money. She would meet other girls in her same situation—Brittany, Nicole, and Danielle— each one a courier in the oxycodone conspiracy.

She would eventually meet John. It was at his home on Saco Street in Dorchester, and there was another meeting at John and Anh's new place on Park Street. John and several others routinely sat at a long table where they dumped stacks of money and dozens, if not hundreds, of vitamin bottles. There were no vitamins in the bottles, however. They had been packed with oxycodone pills and resealed. The process was fairly simple, though time-consuming. The conspirators would peel the original plastic off a vitamin bottle with a razor blade, fill the bottles with the pills, and then, using superglue, they'd adhere the plastic back on. They even kept and carried the receipts for the vitamins they bought, so that just in case they were stopped at an airport, they could claim they were transporting vitamins—a lot of vitamins. Once the pills arrived in Massachusetts, the bottles were reopened, and the pills were counted. Colby Deering, a longtime friend of John's, was often there, too. Deering, thirty-eight years old, had a couple of run-ins with police when he was younger, but had no convictions. He was a bit skittish around drugs, so he sat alone or with the women.

"We'd all count," Nina admits. "It wasn't like a hidden fact or anything. Like, there were a lot of people that, you know, me, Stanley, Johnny, Pete, or whoever, would all count, you know. In the beginning, it would be like, you know, two thousand or three thousand pills at a time. As time went on, there were more and more, though."

More and more pills meant more and more money. The women would separate the cash into stacks of hundreds, fifties, twenties, and tens. A money counter would be used and set to various amounts, but the most common amount was $1,000. In a matter of seconds, fifty $20 bills or other denominations adding up to $1,000 would be counted and wrapped in a thick red rubber band. Five $1,000 stacks would be bound together, so there were easy-to-count bundles of $5,000. The most Nina ever counted at one time was $950,000. The most she ever carried on a plane was $150,000.

"I guess they needed money down in Florida," she said, "and Stanley called me at home and he told me that he had booked me a flight, and I had to go down to Florida."

Nina, who was studying to become a paralegal, would have to skip school that night. Her flight was leaving in ninety minutes, and she had to race from Cape Cod to Logan Airport in Boston. She threw some books and a couple of outfits along with thirty stacks of $5,000 into her suitcase and ran out the door. She knew she was supposed to vacuum-seal the money and hide it in the liner of the suitcase, and then cover it with clothes and other items, but there was no time.

"I was in a rush," she explained. "I figured I'd, you know, when I got to the airport, I'd hide it or something. Stanley would have been really mad if I had missed my flight."

Nina made the flight. She checked the bag with the $150,000 dollars tossed in haphazardly and flew to West Palm Beach. It had been decided previously that the couriers would fly into smaller airports with the running theory that they may be less conspicuous. On this occasion, it worked. Nina was picked up without incident by Pete Melendez in his black Escalade.

Pete drove Nina to the modest home he was living in with Brian Bowes, and searched for the key to unlock the suitcase. John had purchased the locks and insisted they be used because he didn't trust his drug-addicted couriers with large sums of money and pills. Keys to the suitcase locks were kept in both Massachusetts and Florida. When Pete opened the suitcase and saw how the money was packed, he looked disapprovingly at Nina.

"What the hell is this?"

"I was in a rush," Nina said defiantly. "I just kind of threw it in there, I guess."

"You got lucky," Pete said. "Stanley and Johnny would have killed you."

Pete kept his mouth shut about Nina's carelessness with the money, in part because he was too busy celebrating his fiftieth birthday. After counting the money, he brought it to Stanley, who had found a new drug supplier in Miami. With the wheels of the drug deal already in motion, John decided to throw Pete's big birthday bash in South Beach. All the players in the conspiracy were there. Even though she was not part of the conspiracy, Anh flew down from Massachusetts at John's behest. John took everyone out to dinner and then to a club. It was a harmless night of fun and extravagance until a relatively unknown rapper approached Anh at the nightclub. He hit on her. She turned him down. So, he called her the c-word. It all happened very fast. Colby overheard the insult and shoved the man back several feet. Before a fight ensued, the rapper's entourage intervened and held him back. They verbally threatened Colby, who stood his ground, but cooler heads prevailed and the rapper's posse left the club.

A few minutes later, John returned from the men's room and Anh told him what had transpired. John was incensed! He grabbed Gonsalves, who stands about 6-foot-3 and weighs over three hundred pounds, and the two of them ran out to the parking lot. Colby was right behind them and was able to point out the rapper getting into his Mercedes.

"That's him!" Colby shouted.

John and Gonsalves jumped in their car and sped after the unsuspecting rapper. Gonsalves was driving, and he pulled up alongside the Mercedes while John waved his gun out the window. That's when the rapper, who was sitting in the backseat, first realized he was being chased and his life was in danger. Gonsalves swerved toward the Mercedes, and forced it to a stop on the side of the road. John jumped out of the car and ran to the rear passenger door. The rapper hadn't thought to lock the door, and John swung it open forcefully. He grabbed the frightened man, pulled him out of the car, and put the gun to his head. Gonsalves made it clear to the rapper's entourage that they should stay back.

"What did you call my wife?" John shouted.

"I didn't mean nothin' by it," the rapper said with a quivering voice. "Besides, your boy stepped in. Things is cool."

At this point, police sirens could be heard approaching. John turned and saw the flashing blue lights. He popped the rapper in the chin with a closed fist, and tucked the gun under his shirt. When the police arrived, they were told by both sides that nothing had happened. They were all friends who were deciding where to go for the rest of the night.

"I suggest you all go home, and call it a night," one of the officers said.

"Yes, sir," John said respectfully, and then had Gonsalves drive him back to the nightclub.

The next day Colby signed the lease for the home John had picked out to rent in Florida. It was a $2.4 million ranch-style home on the water in Wilton Manors, a suburb of Fort Lauderdale. The house had a large foyer that opened up to a dining room on the left and a living room straight ahead. The living room was flanked by sliding doors that led out to the pool and Jacuzzi. The kitchen was undersized, with an island in the middle. Off the kitchen was a hallway leading to three bedrooms, including a master bedroom with a walk-in closet and glass doors that opened to a small deck overlooking the water.

John planned to headquarter his operation out of the house. Pete and Brian Bowes would live there full-time, and John would stay there during his many trips to the area. In return for putting his name on the lease, Colby would also be able to stay there when he was in Florida, and John would pay for everything, including cars and boats, and food and any other living expenses. All Colby had to do was sign the lease.

At the signing, John and Colby attempted to pay for the first and last month's rent, plus the security deposit, in cash, but the realtor for the landlord wouldn't accept cash, and wouldn't hand over the keys. It took nearly three weeks to complete the deal, but on August 31, John gave $12,000 in cash to the realtor representing him, and that realtor paid the deposit.

It's fairly obvious the owner of the house didn't like the idea of renting to John and his friends, because when the September rent was late by a few days, Colby was immediately served a three-day notice of eviction. Five days later, Colby paid the rent and the $200 late fee with a money order, and was allowed to continue renting the house. However, Colby continued to be behind on the rent and failed to pay for January and February of 2011. He was also simultaneously behind on his own rent for the apartment where he lived in Quincy, Massachusetts. He borrowed money from his boss at the car stereo store, but it wasn't enough.

"I need the money," Colby begged John in an urgent phone call from his apartment in Quincy. "My landlord is really on my ass."

"I sent you the money," John argued. "Where is it? What did you do with it?"

"I didn't get any money," Colby responded. "You have to send me some. I need money!"

"Well, we're not there," John said from Florida. "We can't get it to you right now."

"But I need the money!" Colby exclaimed in desperation. "I need the money!"

"I'll send somebody to get it to you," John said reassuringly. He hung up the phone and called Anh in Dorchester to tell her that Colby needed $3,400 for his rent. Anh pulled the exact amount out of the safe in their apartment and brought it to Colby.

That matter was resolved, but on March 12, 2011, the realtor for the Wilton Manors home discovered that John had moved everyone out of the house two weeks earlier. Brian and Pete, who had been living there full-time, left the house a mess and with the air-conditioning set at sixty degrees. John had decided impulsively to move his operation to another home in Sunrise, Florida. It was a better house right on the Intracoastal Waterway where John could keep his boat and water skis. So, he simply abandoned the other house, the one with Colby's name on the lease. The landlord subsequently sued Colby for the unpaid rent and damages.

John's drug operation grew rapidly. Hundreds of pills became thousands. Tens of thousands of dollars became hundreds of thousands. Alexa remembers counting as many as eleven thousand pills for one transaction. The demand for the pills was high, and the supply was incredibly easy to get. All someone had to do to get a year's worth of painkillers was to have an MRI, and because the MRI machines are portable, the operators of the pill mills simply brought the machines in semitrailers to places where dealers and abusers hang out, such as strip clubs.

The trailers were parked in the back of the clubs, and operators would scan anyone who could hand over $200 to $300. Cars would pull up. Drivers and passengers would get out, have their bodies scanned, and drive away with a prescription for any painkiller of their choosing, which they could easily get at any of South Florida's pill mills.

"It doesn't matter whether the MRI shows an injury," Lt. Bruce Hannan of the Palm Beach County Sheriff's Office told the *Florida Sun Sentinel*. "The doctor just wants something on file, something to cover his ass in case someone checks. The MRI centers are feeding the process and taking advantage."

Gonsalves paid John between $12 and $15 per pill, and then sold them for $20 each to the dealers. Customers ultimately paid $25 to $30. There were a lot of people in the pipeline making a lot of money, and thousands of people from Cape Cod to Boston getting high on and addicted to oxycodone.

"I looked at it this way," John says. "If you can get me ten thousand pieces, I'll give you five thousand dollars above whatever you paid. I don't care if you tell me it comes to a dollar over what you paid. They could make another ten thousand. I said, 'I don't care.' As long as I agree to the price, I don't care what you make. Some of these guys were making fifty thousand dollars every time they saw me. I didn't care."

That's John's way of implying that he wasn't greedy. He didn't try to squeeze every last dollar out of a drug deal. He generously allowed everyone involved to make money. Within months of the operation getting under way, Nina and Gonsalves traded in their used car for a brand-new black Mercedes E500. Melendez and Bowes moved out of their small Florida apartments into the large home on the water. And John went on a bit of a shopping spree of his own. However, it's difficult for a drug dealer without credit cards or a valid driver's license to purchase expensive items. He needed help. Colby Deering became the man behind the man. John and Colby walked into the Russo Marine showroom in Medford, Massachusetts, and browsed for a boat. They each wore jeans and a T-shirt, and when they spent some extra time admiring a twenty-nine-foot 1998 Sea Ray 290 Sundancer, a salesman approached with a handshake and a smile.

"How much is it?" John asked directly. "And don't give me an answer with a lot of words and no answer. How much is it?"

"Twenty-five thousand dollars," the salesman responded obediently.

"All right," John said. "I want it."

Inside a small office in the back, John explained that he didn't like to have his name on documents, and that Colby would be paying for and financing the boat. The salesman didn't ask any questions, nor did he react in any discernibly surprised or confused way when John placed a paper bag full of cash on the salesman's desk. Inside the bag were $10, $20, and $100 bills adding up to a down payment of $2,500. As Colby prepared to sign the ownership papers, Russo Marine asked him routine finance questions and ran a credit report on him. Colby claimed to make $4,500 a month as a car radio installer in Quincy. That may or may not have been true, but his credit score came back too low to complete the sale.

Without any red-faced embarrassment, John used his cell phone to call one of Anh's cousins, Thao Tran. She agreed to sign for the boat, but like Colby, her credit was insufficient. Still undeterred, John left the $2,500 with the salesman and vowed to return. A few days later, he came back with Peter Melendez and another bag of cash. This bag had exactly 1,043 twenty-dollar bills in it—the exact amount needed to pay off the balance of the boat, plus tax. Melendez, the last in a series of proposed straw owners, signed his name on the purchase and sale agreement.

"You realize, of course, Mr. Willis, that the boat will legally belong to Mr. Melendez," the salesman said. He was hoping for an explanation as to why John didn't sign for the boat himself, and he got one.

"I never put anything in my name," John said proudly. "I'm a ghost to the government."

"So, you do everything in cash?" the nosy salesman asked.

"All cash. All the time. All I am is a money man," John said, adding with surprising honesty, "it's what I do. I sell product for cash. I pay for more product with cash."

"What's the product?"

"Oxy," John said without flinching. "People love oxy. They're big into it. And so am I. I don't deal them pills, though. I'm just a money man."

John named the boat *Double Down* and used it for both recreation and to conduct drug deals in the privacy of open waters.

John's next big purchase was a 2005 Bentley Continental GT. The price tag on that was $80,500. After the sales tax and registration fees, John would need to come up with precisely $86,125. He paid for a little more than half of it in cash installments over a period of ten days. The payments of $1,000, $6,000, $13,000, $10,000, and two payments of $8,450 were all made in person and in cash. The money was wrapped in rubber bands and counted by the salesperson. This time, Colby filled out a credit report and claimed to make $9,500 a month, and he was able to sign for and purchase the car.

A few months after he drove it off the lot, John drove drunk and crashed the Bentley into a pole, putting a huge dent in the bumper. The next morning, John was found lying on his couch with a box full of vomit next to him. Because the car was in Colby's name, Colby filed an insurance claim and stated he was the driver. Soon thereafter, Colby cashed a check for $3,243.96 from Arbella Insurance.

"Greed didn't drive me," John contends. "Money doesn't drive me. I like the business. Is it the adrenaline rush? I like the fact that I can do business and take care of my family. I like the fact that I can take care of others. As far as chasing greed, money will come and go. It's not about that. It's about the people around you, and what you do with what you have. I have never looked at money as my God."

John may not have worshiped the almighty dollar, but he certainly enjoyed making it and spending it. He loved feeling like a big shot! He couches it as generosity, a desire to help others or to take care of them, but that doesn't sufficiently explain the cars, the boats, the jewelry, and the houses he bought for himself. Yes, he liked to take care of people, in part because it sufficiently fed his ego by placing him above the people he supported. Money and power made the orphaned high school dropout feel smart. And that was important. He wanted the same status that better educated people—doctors, lawyers, businessmen—achieved. His physical prowess and his conviction to do what needed to be done were never in question, but he feared his intelligence was, and it wasn't enough for John to be the strongest man in the room, or the one with the most money. His insatiable ego required him to see himself, and for others to see him, as the strongest and the most powerful, handsome, generous, and intelligent one in the group. It would never be enough to be one or two of those things. He needed to be all of them.

"I've been involved in a lot of things," John says. "I've learned a lot. One thing I can't say: I can't say that I'm naive or dumb. I find it very insulting, even when people are joking, when they say I'm dumb. I'm not dumb. I've been there and done that, you know what I mean? These people I work with are very intelligent. We've all made a lot of money. Intelligence and money are always gonna win the game, you know."

John had both intelligence and money, but he would ultimately lose the game because he was also both arrogant and self-destructive. Additionally, there seemed to be an element of willful ignorance at play. John knew he was being followed by the FBI, but instead of seeing it as a warning sign, he reveled in the excitement of speeding down Monsignor O'Brien Highway in Cambridge and crossing over three lanes of traffic on Storrow Drive, and then looking in his rearview mirror and realizing he had lost the car following him.

"Idiots," he thought to himself.

When he was stopped at Logan Airport and his money was seized—that was a warning. When authorities stopped him again and took his diamond watch—that was a warning. When two other accomplices were stopped by police and had a grand total of sixty-two pounds of pot seized—that was another warning. When he sat at a blackjack table in a Florida casino and an FBI agent sat down next to him and played a few hands—that was more than a warning. That was a declaration that the feds knew where he was, knew what he was up to, and were on a mission to prove it.

"I was aware they were following me around," John says. "But I always thought I wasn't doing anything. So, they weren't going to catch me with any drugs, bombs, or nonsense. I don't even exist. I don't exist in the tax life. I don't exist in the work life. My nightclub, my liquor store, my brother. He's not my real brother, so there's no real connection to me. There's no trail. On my cars, I don't register any of the insurances. So, who am I? Nobody. There is nothing they can prove to get me. Nothing. But they don't need to prove it. That's the problem."

In truth, the FBI had enough evidence to prove a case against John very early in its investigation, but they wanted to know the magnitude of his criminal activities, and his connection to two other known criminals, Ming Jai and Wei Xing Chen. Ming Jai had been a member of Ping On in the 1990s, and briefly vied for control when Sky Dragon fled. According to the FBI, Wei Xing Chen was an Asian organized crime figure who ran brothels and gambling dens. The following is from an affidavit submitted in November of 2010 by FBI Special Agent Timothy C. McElroy:

"We have not yet achieved significant goals of the investigation, which include, among other things, identifying all participants in the subject criminal enterprise; the nature and location of all the targets' activities; with regard to the drug business, the total amounts of money and drugs being exchanged by members of the subject organization; all of the routes and methods of transportation used by the targets and their connections to move narcotics into and through Massachusetts and to move money out of Massachusetts.

"Specifically, with regard to the criminal activities of WILLIS…I believe that WILLIS was sending money to Florida in furtherance of the Percocet scheme…Regarding that scheme, we have not identified WILLIS's immediate source of drugs; the identities of the users of the phones involved; their ultimate sources; the means and routes of transportation for the drugs; and how the money is paid to suppliers and the doctor(s) involved.

"With regard to extortion...it may be that WILLIS is simply a collector for MING JAI in his role as an enforcer in the Asian community, or it may be that WILLIS has some kind of partnership with MING JAI."

The FBI had its questions, and soon they would have their answers. As their case was building, John's criminal empire was crumbling. There were plenty of opportunities for John to run, or to get out of the drug business, but he considered neither option. He remained careful in the conduct of his business, but conducting the business with the FBI watching was by definition reckless. Still, like an addict, John couldn't stop.

"My mother told me," John recalls, "you can never take the spots off a leopard. Can I change when I'm forty what I've been doing since I was fourteen? If this is who I am, and I'm okay with it, why am I going to change that?"

He was about to find out.

TEN

ON NOVEMBER 28, 2010, Kimberly and Lilly Nguyen were laid to rest. It was warm for a late fall New England day. The sun shone brightly, and the sky was azure blue. Hundreds of mourners packed St. Ambrose Church in Dorchester to pay their respects to the lovely young sisters. Tony Nguyen escorted his twelve-year-old daughter, Stephanie, who clutched a framed photograph of her mother. Sunglasses hid Stephanie's tears, and a white headscarf made her look much older than she was.

John, one of only a few white faces in the congregation, sat with Anh. While she mourned, he sat stoically. He held Anh's hand, gave a faint smile to familiar relatives and friends, and nodded his agreement when he heard the priest shout from the altar about senseless violence. There was no irony in John's response, because he had always opposed violence if it didn't have a rational purpose.

He leaned forward in the pew and put his head down. Anyone observing him would think he was genuinely sad, but John was busy plotting and scheming. Several fires had broken out in his oxycodone-trafficking business in just the past month, and each of them needed his attention. His mind darted from one crisis to another like a mosquito bouncing on a pond. One by one he found a solution to each of his problems. John always seemed to know what to do. What he didn't know was that the FBI was waiting for him outside the church. John had recently, and quite accidentally, become the subject of an investigation. The FBI had him under surveillance ever since they witnessed him making a bag transfer after leaving a brothel in Cambridge.

"That's when we were off and running on Willis," FBI Special Agent Russell Chisholm says.

Chisholm was a local kid. He grew up in Quincy and walked many of the same streets as John, but he followed a very different path out. He spent thirteen years in the United States Army, and then joined the FBI in 1995. He started in the white-collar crimes unit, moved to terrorism investigations, and then to organized crime. His focus for several years was Russian organized crime, but in 2009, he was assigned to investigate the Asians. Within a year, the FBI was closely watching the gambling dens and brothels in and around Boston and Chinatown. They were gathering evidence of prostitution, human trafficking, extortion, and drug dealing. No part of the investigation touched John until he drove up to that Cambridge brothel in his red Hummer. FBI agents were there, and they took notice.

"They bootstrapped me into an investigation," John complains. "That's the only way they could get the infiltration into what I was doing. So what did they do? They went in front of a grand jury and said, 'Well, this guy is involved. He's this. He's that. He's the enforcer. He's the boss.' I mean, which is it? Am I the boss, or am I the enforcer? But they got the wiretaps. And through their wiretaps, what did they get? They got no information, but somehow they got a continuance of the wiretap every thirty days. So then they finally stumbled on to my business in Florida, and they see this vast amount of money I'm making. I always assumed my phones were tapped, but I thought by switching them, I'd be all right. This is the problem. If you have a phone and they tap it, because they think you're doing something wrong, more power to them, but if they tap six phones in the hopes that one of them is your number, and none of them is in your name, I don't think they have a right to do that. The government gets away with it."

The brothel John went into belonged to a naturalized U.S. citizen named Wei Chen, known to police as a significant Asian organized crime figure. Chen had been operating at least three houses of prostitution since 2005, and was convicted of it in 2007 after Boston police raided his brothel at 49 Pratt Street in Allston and found condoms, lubricants, cell phones, and $7,500 in cash.

Told by a confidential informant that Chen was at it again, the FBI began its investigation. They quickly discovered the informant was credible, and that Chen trusted him. Equipped with a recording device taped under his shirt, the informant sat with Chen inside Chen's brothel at 185 Charles Street in Cambridge.

"You were busted in New York," Chen said to the informant, "when my whorehouse got busted. Fuck, if you can stand in the kitchen, you can take the heat. Right? Am I right? Like me, what the fuck am I doing? Fuck, I am breaking the law, but I'm not breaking any major law. I'm just opening a whorehouse. Fuck, what kind of law am I breaking? There's nothing."

So, the FBI knew quickly that Chen had returned to the business of prostitution. Soon they would also find that Chen had become a midlevel narcotics dealer specializing in marijuana and Ecstasy. The informant drove up from New York to Boston with Chen's cousin Tong and another man named Ah-Kay. While Tong went to Ah-Kay's Chinatown apartment to pick up the drugs, the informant left them to meet up with FBI agents, who put a wire on him again. The informant returned to make the buy, where he overheard Tong telling Chen they were short six hundred pills.

"Short six hundred?" Chen asked, surprised.

"Only 2,407 pills," Tong explained. "That means it's 593 short."

"You go ahead and give him," Chen said. "That's all I got."

"Yes. Good."

The case against Chen was building quickly. The FBI now had enough to get a warrant to tap Chen's phone, which is when they first heard John's voice. On October 27, 2010, the FBI listened as John volunteered to beat up a couple of unknown Malaysians. One of Chen's employees had gone to a karaoke bar in Quincy and was attacked in the bathroom.

"Who beat him up?" John asked in Cantonese. "What's his name? I want to get the son of a bitch! Where is he right now?"

"The kid knows," Chen answered. "He will take you there. You get him!"

John didn't regularly work as Chen's enforcer, but he frequented Chen's brothels and gambling dens and wasn't averse to doing him a favor. There's no evidence that John followed through with his threat to beat up the Malaysian, but a few days later, Chen's employee was attacked again. This time the employee was hit over the head with a bottle, presumably by the same Malaysian attacker. So, Chen had another employee deliver the message that if the attacks didn't stop, he would have the Malaysian "whacked." It's uncertain, but also unlikely, that the threat was ever carried out.

"What they got me on was the idea of a threat," John complains. "Because I said I would go take care of something. I never hurt nobody. I never did anything. They say, 'We know Mr. Willis gets money through extortionate means. We don't know who, why, or when, or for whom.' Mind you, I'm making a hundred forty grand a week doing my own thing. Why would I bother to extort anyone?"

But John had stumbled into the middle of an FBI investigation. The feds were really after Chen, and Chen unknowingly led them to another organized crime figure named Ming Jai, and John was an acquaintance of both men. In fact, John had known Ming Jai for nearly thirty years. Ming Jai, not to be confused with Bai Ming, John's longtime boss, was a member of Ping On under Stephen Tse (Sky Dragon), and had vied for control of the gang when Tse fled to China. When Ming Jai's efforts proved inadequate, he opted to head up the Kam Shing Gang in Brooklyn, New York. In 1997, he was sentenced to seven years for heroin trafficking. The subsequent term of supervised release ended in 2009, and he returned to Boston and resumed his criminal activities in January of 2010.

By October of 2010, the FBI had received warrants for wiretaps on several phones used by Chen, Ming Jai, and John's oldest friend from the Ping On days, Woping Joe, who worked as a card dealer in the gambling dens. Within weeks there were wiretaps on several of John's phones and those of his accomplices. The FBI's small investigation into Chen's brothels quickly mushroomed into a large-scale investigation into Chen's vast criminal activities, Ming Jai's gambling operation, and John's drug trafficking.

"We had reports that Willis was smuggling pills out of Florida," FBI Special Agent Chisholm contends. "Originally, the case was all about prostitution, gambling, and extortion."

The wiretaps on Ming Jai's phones were especially incriminating. On one recording he was referred to as "White Powder Ming." On another he could be heard telling his girlfriend, Huyen Truong, that two gamblers had lost nearly $100,000, and that nearly half of that was "water money," which is commissions paid to the gambling den. Transcripts of other phone calls would prove to be equally damning.

"Hey, Kehro, it's about time for you to call me back," Ming Jai told one debtor in Chinese. "Don't be so strange. Let's respect each other. Fuck your mother, don't think that when you don't answer your phone, you are taking care of fucking things. I'll definitely find you. You shouldn't take me for a fucking fool."

In another conversation, Kehro pleaded for more time to make restitution, but Ming Jai responded by making explicit threats.

"I already got one person yesterday," Ming Jai said. "Let me tell you that I don't want you to be the second one. I know your people. You weren't like this. One person came under my knife only yesterday."

"Definitely I wouldn't be the second one," Kehro replied.

"Fuck, I'm most fucking mad at people who come to get my fucking money," Ming Jai shouted. "You fuck! I don't care how you pay me. Fuck your mother. You enter my website to gamble. I saw that. You said you went to a bank, but you wouldn't answer your phone. Fuck, the moment you say you wouldn't pay me. Fuck your mother. Just see what I do."

"Don't be so mad," Kehro pleaded.

"Fuck, you ought to see the Vietnamese kid that I got only yesterday," Ming Jai threatened again. "I got him under the knife. I want to let you know that. I don't want you to be the second one."

"Give me two more weeks," Kehro negotiated. "I'll definitely be able to take care of it for you."

"If you say so, then I won't make any fucking calls," Ming Jai said, referring to calling his enforcer, Hin Pau, to collect the money. "At the end of this month, I want to see the money. That's all the fucking thing I want to say."

In another phone call with one of his employees, Ming Jai explained that he was looking for a guy who owed him $600.

"This bastard," Ming Jai began. "It's not because of the meager six hundred dollars. I just want to beat up the son of a bitch."

"I wish I could help you find him," the employee said, "but I can't, because he owes me money, too. I told him if he comes out, I'll definitely beat him to death."

In an effort to collect a few hundred dollars from another gambler named Ken, Ming Jai left this voice mail: "Let me tell you, if you don't take my call, your whole family will go to hell. I am telling you."

In April of 2011, Ming Jai had coronary bypass surgery at Boston Medical Center. Two stents were installed to improve blood circulation around his heart. From his hospital bed, he continued doing business.

"Hey, Peter, you motherfucker!" Ming Jai shouted into his tapped phone. "If you really don't want to answer my phone calls, and if I happen to beat you up, don't complain that I haven't showed you enough courtesy. When you took my money to gamble, fuck, I loaned it to you. I was very fucking quick in loaning you the money. If you think the best is not to answer my fucking phone calls, then when I get to beat you up, you motherfucker, I'm just going to do it."

Despite his apparent enthusiasm, Ming Jai was also recorded cautioning his enforcer, Hin Pau, that beating up too many gambling customers would be bad for business, because the victims might go to the police or be lost as customers.

This admonition was given a short time after Hin Pau had a confrontation with a Vietnamese man in the Beach Street gambling den about an unpaid debt. As the argument escalated, Hin Pau told one of his associates to go get a "piece of metal," meaning a gun, and the Vietnamese man promised in a shaky voice that he would make good on his debt.

On May 24, 2011, the Boston Police Department raided Ming Jai's gambling den at 17-23 Beach Street in Chinatown. They detained Ming Jai and Bai Ming along with two other employees, but allowed the forty-three gamblers in the den to leave with the money in their hands and in their pockets. The police seized a total of $27,616 from the pai gow table and from a cabinet in Ming Jai's office. They also took scoring sheets, ledgers, and computer printouts. They had caught Ming Jai red-handed. A similar fate would befall Wei Chen.

Again, the wiretaps on the phones provided a wealth of information to investigators. Wei Chen was taped having several conversations with Ah-Kay, who ran Chen's brothel on Everett Street in Allston. In one conversation, Ah-Kay said he was optimistic that a customer named David would show up despite the rain, because Ah-Kay had told him that this "Hong Kong girl would be right for him, because she had large breasts." In another conversation, Ah-Kay explained to Wei Chen that he couldn't close up the brothel because "White Devil John is here and will not leave." And in yet another, Wei Chen told a man named Yang to have sex with one of the new girls to introduce her to her new life as a prostitute.

As authorities continued to intercept phone calls, they learned that the going rate for a prostitute at one of Wei Chen's brothels was $130 plus tips; that Wei Chen placed ads in Chinese-language newspapers to get women to work as prostitutes; that he regularly transported women across state lines to engage in prostitution, often by force; and that Wei Chen was additionally engaged in trafficking controlled substances, including marijuana.

"The merchandise sells for thirty-eight or thirty-nine," investigators heard Wei Chen say. "The stuff is very good. It smells good with a good fragrance."

One customer in particular was not so easily convinced. Forty-five-year-old Mark Mataev of West Roxbury asked Wei Chen to give him a sample, and if he liked it, he would come back and buy more. Wei Chen agreed and Mataev later bought a pound of marijuana for $4,000. Mataev was then spotted by a Boston police officer smoking a joint inside his car in front of Boston University's Agganis Arena on Commonwealth Avenue. The officer searched the car and found the large bag of pot. Mataev would later explain in the presence of his lawyers that he had bought the pot from Wei Chen, whom he called "Jeff," and that Jeff was an Asian man in his forties who drove a silver Mercedes. Mataev also confirmed for the FBI that Wei Chen operated brothels in Cambridge, Allston, and Medford. That was the first the FBI had heard about a brothel in Medford.

John preferred the brothel in Cambridge. He liked the assortment of women there, and if he wasn't happy, he knew the girls would be rotated out every ten days and new girls would be brought in. He was at the Cambridge brothel on November 5, 2010. Surveillance agents observed him going in at 1:35 in the afternoon, and watched him leave at 2:05. Because Willis was a known criminal with no visible means of support, but was driving a $40,000 Hummer, they decided to follow him.

Meanwhile, about twenty minutes after John left Chen's brothel, Chen called an Asian male named Hoi Shen while the FBI listened in.

"I have some merchandise I need you to take care of for me," Hoi Shen said.

"Is it the same stuff as before?" Chen asked.

"Yes, it's good stuff."

"Okay," Chen said. "I'll do what I can, but that fucking Caucasian has ruined my connection to the Vietnamese guy. The Caucasian used to be good, but now he won't take my calls."

The FBI assumed the Caucasian was John, and that he had begun dealing directly with the unidentified Vietnamese guy, thereby cutting out Chen.

At six o'clock, John drove down Harrison Avenue in South Boston and pulled up alongside a red Chevrolet sedan. The car was rented by Colby Deering, who is a white man, and it was a white man who got out of the red sedan. However, it is unclear if it was Deering who met John that day.

The unidentified male had a brief conversation with John, and then went to the rear of the Hummer and took out a large black suitcase. The suitcase was placed in the trunk of the Chevy, and the driver followed John to Chinatown. As John drove, he texted and made phone calls from what the FBI referred to as Target Telephone #4. In the span of nine minutes, John made one phone call and sent eight text messages. By the end of the day, he would make and send a combined ninety-three calls and text messages from phone #4. John had as many as five cell phones at one time, and it seemed clear to the FBI that he was using #4 to conduct a drug deal.

John and the man driving the Chevy arrived in Chinatown in their separate cars and met an Asian man, Aibun Eng, driving a white Honda Odyssey minivan. Eng, suspected by police of being a drug dealer, retrieved the black suitcase from the back of the car and waited.

Two hours later, a black man named Andrew Alicea drove up to Eng's van in a Lincoln Continental SUV. Alicea, known to be an associate of Eng's, went to the back of the van and pulled out a dark bag, different from the black suitcase. He then drove his Lincoln to an underground parking garage and returned five minutes later. Alicea and Eng drove away separately, and within a few minutes, Alicea was stopped on Herald Street by Boston police.

"Do you have a gun on you?" the officer asked as he walked up to Alicea's window.

"No," Alicea said, "not on me."

"Do you have a gun in the vehicle?"

"Yes."

The police searched the car and found two pounds of marijuana and a handgun. Alicea was arrested, but he refused to cooperate. Meanwhile, Eng was stopped and his minivan was also searched. Police recovered sixty pounds of pot inside the black suitcase that was first in John's possession. Eng also refused to answer questions.

John took the news in stride. He was just as unconcerned about the loss of sixty pounds of pot as he was a few weeks earlier when police confiscated nearly $14,000 from him at Logan Airport. On that day, John attempted to board a plane to Fort Lauderdale with a fake driver's license. He had been flying with the fake ID for nearly two years, but this time he got caught. TSA officials pulled him aside and called the Massachusetts State Police in to question him.

"Where are you going, Mr. Willis?" an officer asked.

"Fort Lauderdale," John answered.

"Well, you know there's a big pill problem in South Florida."

"Yeah, what's that got to do with me?" John asked innocently. "I don't do pills."

"How about I take a look at your cell phone?" the officer inquired.

"Why?"

"Because I think you're a drug dealer."

"You think I'm a drug dealer," John said, leaning in. "How about this? I've been convicted for it. So, you're right. But I don't have any drugs on me now. So, what's the problem?"

"Well, I just need to look at your phone to see if you're selling drugs today," the officer persisted.

"First of all, you need a subpoena to look at my phone," John said. "You're not looking at my phone."

"What are you, a tough guy?" the officer asked, and in the silence he observed how calm and cavalier John was. Most of the people he'd dealt with in a similar situation acted nervously. It was strange to see John appear so unconcerned.

During the consensual interview, John explained to the police that he had purchased his plane ticket the day before, because he was in trouble with his two girlfriends and needed to leave town in a hurry. He told them he was a personal trainer who dabbled in real estate on the side, and that the cash he had on him was his life savings. None of it was true.

"Am I under arrest?" John asked abruptly.

"No, not today," the officer said. "But we'll be keeping this wad of cash, because you can't explain how you came by it legally."

The officer rifled through a thick wad of bills, mostly twenties and hundreds, that added up to $3,990.

"Well, I need a cab," John said, and he snatched a $20 from the officer's hand and walked out. Meanwhile, John's checked luggage was already on its way to Fort Lauderdale. Officials there searched the bag, and while there were no drugs in it, the K-9 dog alerted positively to the bag, indicating it had previously contained drugs. Another $9,600 was seized. But John wasn't arrested.

"No, they don't arrest you," he explains. "See, that's just how you get to understand the government. If it were such a crime, they would arrest, right? But they just take your money, and then you gotta prove to them that it's yours. What if you saved your money since you were twelve years old, and you come up with fifty thousand? You drive down the street with the money you saved, and they ask you where you got it. If you can't prove you've been saving it since you were twelve, the government confiscates it and keeps it. It's their way of harassing you. They don't arrest you. They take your money, and you've gotta fight for your money back."

It's a sound hypothetical argument with no basis in reality, because John hadn't been saving the money since he was a child. He was a drug dealer, and the FBI was working on a case to prove it. They stopped him again a few weeks later when John got off an airplane in South Florida. Two Broward County police officers patted John down as he passed through security. One of the officers picked up his bag after it had been scanned, and said, "Do you mind if I search your bag?"

"Go ahead," John said casually. "You won't find anything."

But they did find a watch encrusted with thirty-seven karats in diamonds. John estimated its value at $150,000.

"Wow! This is a nice watch!" one of the officers said. "What does something like this cost?"

"It's not mine," John lied. "It's a gift for somebody. I'm trying to sell it for a jeweler."

The officer smiled, offering the slightest indication that he knew John was lying. This was part of the game John didn't enjoy, but he didn't mind playing. He was reminded again about the prescription pill market being very big business in South Florida, and that there were a lot of illegal drug dealers making their way in and out of the state. John did his best to exude ignorance and innocence, and even though the police weren't buying it, they kept the watch and let John go.

John never petitioned to get the money from the first seizure or the diamond watch from the second returned to him. It was simply the cost of doing business, and business was still extremely good, but each encounter with authorities left John more bitter, paranoid, and cynical.

"They do it to destroy lives," John begins his rant. "And what does it all come down to? It comes down to the legalization of taxation. That's all it is. Same as Prohibition. The FBI was founded on Prohibition. That's all the FBI was—a legalized mob. They had the right to kill. And that's what they did to get their money, to get the tax money, and to stop these people from making the money behind the government's back. That's the truth. Any kind of organization, my organized crime, you know, what were we doing? Were we making money? Sure. Were we taxed on it? No. They taxed it in the beginning, because there were prescription meds. Wasn't enough, though. They seen other people making money. No good. Same thing. Chinatown? Same thing. Gangsters making money through gambling. Where's the money? Why are we not getting our cut? Let's break that up. You know what I mean? That's just how it goes."

Back home in Boston, John spent some time around the Chinatown brothels and gambling dens, and then drove down to Foxwoods Casino in Connecticut, where, according to player rating records, he visited ninety-one times in 2009 and 2010, and had a total buy-in of just under $330,000.

"That's one casino," John brags. "I gambled at six casinos. I've sat there with $487,000 in front of me playing baccarat. Anybody in their right mind would have gotten up and walked away. I started with 26K. I stayed and gambled until I lost all but 98K. And then I thought to myself, 'I'm bored.' And I got up and walked away. I was still up."

On November 8, 2010, he gambled with $13,800, and lost all but $200 of it. The next day John was at Ming Jai's gambling den on Beach Street in Chinatown. Like any other patron, John rang the bell, looked up at the closed-circuit TV camera, and was buzzed in through the locked metal gate. He walked up two flights of stairs past several more cameras and opened the entrance door with the sign reading "Hoi Ping Association Club." Once inside, John was disappointed to see there were no card games or pai gow being played. He didn't stay long, but his arrival sparked a conversation between Ming Jai and the FBI's informant.

"Willis went to Wonder Bar with Woping Joe two weeks ago," the informant said.

"Why do I care?" Ming Jai asked, disinterested.

"Woping Joe says Willis is making a lot of money dealing drugs."

"Good, I hope he brings it here to gamble," Ming Jai said. "He not very good gambler."

John was indeed back at the gambling den two days later. He sat at the pai gow table with Woping Joe and his longtime friend Brant Welty. About three dozen restaurant workers, old ladies, and gangsters were there, too. It was a comparatively low-stakes gambling day for John, who seemed more relaxed than usual. He talked freely and laughed loudly. Ming Jai asked if it was true that John was driving a $130,000 Bentley.

"Yeah, I got one of those," John said. "And a big red Hummer. And I still can't keep any of my bitches happy."

John spoke in a booming voice and his comment drew laughter from everyone in the parlor. He spoke much more softly later when he told Woping Joe and Brant about the big deal he was working on with Bai Ming. The FBI informant was also close enough to hear, and John's voice was very clear on the secret tape recording. Obviously, John knew and trusted the informant, but he didn't know that the informant had agreed to cooperate with the feds in exchange for a lighter sentence in a pending case against him. Still, much of what the FBI had on John to this point was hearsay and circumstantial. The investigators knew what they were after, but they didn't have a strong case yet. That would take quite a while.

Over the next five months, investigators would come to believe that John Willis was the head of a large oxycodone distribution ring based out of Florida and Boston. The investigators watched and listened, and they eventually learned that members of the conspiracy acquired large amounts of oxycodone in Florida and shipped the pills up to Boston, where they were sold in wholesale quantities. The investigators followed the money back to Florida and discovered how it was laundered.

The most frequent courier of both pills and money was a twenty-two-year-old woman from Pawtucket, Rhode Island, named Apponi Malloy. She is a former exotic dancer and adult film star, and also a former neighbor of John's when they both lived in North Providence, Rhode Island, in 2005. She was working as an assistant manager at a restaurant in Rhode Island when John gave her a call. They met at Marina Bay in Quincy, where John docked his boat and kept his jet ski. After a day in the sun, John took Apponi to a sushi restaurant, where Brant Welty was waiting.

Brant was an unexpected participant in the drug conspiracy. He had never been convicted of a crime and had a long history of steady employment, but he had been victimized by the financial crisis. The Alpha Omega Jewelry chain where he worked for seventeen years went bankrupt in January of 2008. Banks seized its assets, and the entire multimillion-dollar inventory was sold. All its stores closed. Brant was out of a job, but he had saved nearly enough money to go into business for himself. With $70,000 coming from John, Brant opened CRU Wine & Spirits, a small liquor store in the South End of Boston, in the fall of 2008. Now, a year later, business was not booming. Perhaps out of desperation, he moved to the wrong side of the law. He would eventually bring his younger sister, Bridget Welty, into the scheme, but for now, his and John's target was Apponi Malloy.

"You wouldn't believe how easy it is to get pills from Florida," John began.

"What kind of pills?" As a longtime user of pot, cocaine, Ecstasy, Percocet, and Vicodin, Apponi was interested.

"Little blues," John said.

"What's that?"

"Oxy," Brant chimed in.

"Is it dangerous?" Apponi asked.

"Easiest thing you'll ever do," John said with a grin. "It's a foolproof plan. Basically, you'd be my personal assistant. You'll fly down to Florida with cash, and then come back with vitamin bottles filled with little blues."

Apponi wanted to think about it. To help her think, John slid an envelope across the table and told her that was just to help her out. Inside the envelope was $2,000 cash.

"I can take care of you," John said sincerely. Then as the conversation continued, he promised to get her a car, a Gucci bag, and breast implants. He vowed not only to "take care of her" regarding rent, bills, and other needs, but also to pay her $500 every time she flew. And over the next eight months, Apponi flew to and from Florida two dozen times.

While the federal investigation was ongoing, she traveled back and forth from Florida and Boston once a week, each time transporting at least one thousand 30-milligram pills of oxycodone. Several times she returned from Florida with up to five thousand pills. She traveled by plane and by car and carried anywhere from $15,000 to $45,000 in cash on every occasion.

"Depending on the time of day," Apponi explains, "I would receive a phone call from either John or Brant telling me that I needed to pack and that I was flying. I was either trying to make the last flight or make the first flight the next morning. At that time I would start packing. I would then get a phone call or a text message, because the way I bought the plane tickets was with a Green Dot card. And with the

Green Dot card, to put money on it you would have to go to CVS or Walgreens, get a charge card, and put the money on it. I would then purchase my plane ticket. I would then have to go up to Boston, either to John's apartment or to Brant's apartment, and then I would have to pack the money."

The cash she took with her was initially rolled up in her clothes, but later, as John and Brant grew more paranoid, they showed Apponi how to vacuum-seal the money so the cash would lie flatter. During her eight months in the drug conspiracy, Apponi met all of the other key figures in the scheme. There was Brant and his younger sister, Bridget Welty; Colby Deering; Michael Shaw, who was known as "Hillbilly" because of his thick Southern accent; Mark Thompson; Steven Le; Vincent Alberico; Kevin Baranowski; Gonsalves; Melendez; the good-looking one, Michael Clemente, whom they called "Ricky Martin"; and Brian Bowes, whom Apponi nicknamed "Avatar."

"Why did you call him Avatar?" she was asked.

"Because he has a dent in the middle of his forehead."

Apponi frequently counted pills with Brant and Bridget, picked up cash from John, and stayed with Shrek and Avatar in Florida. Most of her trips were uneventful, and she began to believe it was indeed a foolproof plan as John had indicated, but a few problems began to arise.

First, she was sent to Florida to meet one of Colby's connections. Colby told her he had never met the supplier, but he knew his brother. Before Apponi's flight, she met Colby at a Ramada Inn in Dorchester, where they spent an hour counting and bagging some pills. The drug trafficking conspiracy had become a family affair, so one of the coconspirator's brothers arrived and paid $20,000 for the pills. Apponi took that money to Tampa. Upon her arrival, she called John to let him know she arrived without incident, and then she called Colby, who told her to wait outside the airport and his connection would be around shortly. A few minutes later, a silver Chrysler drove up, and the black man driving told her to get in.

"I got into the car," Apponi says. "We got a hotel, and then we went all over the place picking up pills."

Apponi and the black man went to more than a dozen pain clinics and a few rundown apartments to find addicts looking to sell a portion of their pills so they could go back out and buy more. Once Apponi and her connection had enough pills, they returned to the hotel, where Apponi rubbed several of them with a black cloth. If the pills smudged, they were likely to be fake.

"So I was doing that," Apponi recalls. "I was checking the codes, like the letter and the numbers on the pills and everything. Come to find out that they were real, so I was able to make the exchange with the black kid for the pills, for the money, packed up my bag, and then I left."

Apponi flew back to Boston that day and gave the pills to Brant. It was his job to then distribute the pills in wholesale amounts to the conspiracy's midlevel customers.

Apponi would return to Tampa a few weeks later, this time with $28,000 that John had given her. She went to pick up the money at John's apartment, but he wasn't there. He had temporarily moved out and was staying at a Sheraton Hotel because he feared the police were watching him. Apponi knocked on the apartment door for quite a while before calling John. When she did call him, he was upset that she was at the apartment. He swore at her several times before Anh, who was with him at the hotel, was able to calm him down. John told Apponi to hurry over to the Sheraton. When Apponi got to the hotel, Anh answered the door and John got up from the bed and handed Apponi a computer bag.

"Be very careful with this," John cautioned. "There's a very expensive laptop in here."

Apponi understood. When she returned to her home to pack, she discovered what she had expected. No laptop, but plenty of cash. Apponi, still very much an addict and an alcoholic, drank heavily the night before her second trip to Tampa. Consequently, she was extremely hungover. When she landed and the black man whose name she never learned picked her up at the airport, she begged him to take her someplace to eat. He pulled into a Burger King and Apponi went inside. She grabbed her purse, but she left the suitcase full of money in the car. When she came out of the restaurant, the car, the man, and the money were gone.

Still too hungover to express much emotion, Apponi called Brant, who called John, who called Colby, who spoke with Apponi a half dozen times in the next few hours. She and Colby both had a phone number for the black man, but he had shut it off or ditched his phone. There wasn't much chance of getting the money back. John was upset about the robbery, but only moderately so. He told Apponi he was sincerely glad she didn't get hurt. His trust in her remained, but that would change.

Apponi's involvement in the conspiracy ended on March 22, 2011, when she delivered 4,200 pills to Vincent Alberico and he was arrested immediately after the exchange. The other members of the conspiracy assumed she had become an informant for the police. What they didn't know was that on that day police had Alberico under surveillance. They watched him drive his powder-blue Corvette to a CVS parking lot in Dorchester, where he met with John, who had arrived in a black Porsche Cayenne. The police observed John getting out of his car and taking a small bag from Alberico, and then they followed Alberico as he drove a few miles down the Southeast Expressway to the South Shore Plaza in Braintree. That's where Alberico met Apponi at a 99 Restaurant.

"He gave me the money," Apponi said. "And then I gave him the pills, and we went our separate ways."

Apponi maintains she did as she was told. She bagged up the pills, threw them in a shoebox, and handed the shoebox to Alberico. As far as she was concerned, her job was done, and she drove home to Rhode Island.

Alberico left the mall and headed south on Route 3 with the State Police right behind. They did a wall-off stop at an exit ramp in Kingston and pulled Alberico over. He jumped out of the car and ran to the trunk in an effort to destroy the evidence. The cops, not knowing what was in the trunk, and thinking Alberico might be rushing to get a gun, jumped Alberico and broke his nose. The scuffle ended with Alberico falling to the ground and bleeding profusely from his nose. The officers took the pills valued at $125,000 out of the trunk, and placed Alberico under arrest. They took him first to Jordan Hospital in Plymouth for treatment, and then to jail.

"Kid Vinnie got pinched," Willis told Brant Welty with investigators listening in on their phone conversation. "He got in a high-speed chase and got pinched on Route 3."

"What happened?"

"I met him," John continued. "He gave me half the money, and then he met Home Girl, and she gave him things. I don't know. Something wrong happened after that."

John, who always referred to the pills as either "things" or "work," shared the news with Brant as if he were giving him a weather report. There was no trace of agitation and no hint of accusation toward Apponi.

"I received a phone call from John asking me if I saw anything suspicious, if I got pulled over, if anything was going on," Apponi explains. "And I told him nothing happened to me. I went on. I went back to my apartment, got relaxed, and then I went to Patriot's Place in Foxboro, and I never saw anything suspicious. I didn't get pulled over. Nothing happened."

Despite the fact that it would make all the sense in the world for the police to have Alberico, a known drug dealer working with John, under surveillance, John's crew considered it suspicious that Alberico would be stopped, but not Apponi.

"They started saying that I was a rat and that I was working for the feds and everything," Apponi says sadly. "So at that point in time I cut all ties with everybody."

She never got the Gucci bag, the car, or the boob job. And two months later she was stopped for driving a stolen vehicle. It was a rental car that John had been paying for, but he stopped payments, and the car was presumed stolen.

"As far as Apponi goes," John says, "she didn't steal. I was just too trusting in her, and she did turn out to be untrustworthy. Unfortunately, as human beings we always go with the thought that we want to go with even when we have contradictory thoughts. At times I'm very stubborn, holding on to my first thought, but as funny as it sounds, you should always trust your first instinct. When you don't, you're always gonna pay for it. Just like now, my first thought when I started this, I had an idea, don't use gangsters, use people that are normal, everyday people who they'll never look at, but my first thought was that if something happens, they're going to tell. But I figured, if I treat them well and I give them money and I treat them like they're family—maybe they won't tell. The most important part of that whole sentence is 'maybe.' When you're betting your life on 'maybe,' shit happens."

John held a similar thought the day he sat in the church at the funeral of the Nguyen sisters. As his head hung low, he pensively ran down the list of recent incidents, run-ins with the law, and money seizures, and wondered whether his gang of coconspirators would hold up if push came to shove. He also began to fully grasp that the feds were after him. He sat in the pew knowing it had been a bad few weeks for his drug business, but he had no idea it was about to get a lot worse.

ELEVEN

EXACTLY ONE WEEK after Anh's aunts were murdered in their home, John was in an Asian grocery picking up bok choy, snow peas, celery, hoisin sauce, and noodles for that night's dinner. He lingered in the aisles of the market because the rain outside was falling heavily, and he was hoping it would taper off by the time he left the store. To delay even longer, John decided to make a long-distance phone call from one of his five cell phones.

"Hey," he said to one of his drug connections in Florida. "My man is leaving tomorrow to go back down to Miami. I'm gonna have him call you when he gets in, and he's gonna give you some money, okay?"

The man John was referring to was Brian Bowes, who was scheduled to fly from Logan Airport to Miami on Spirit Airlines on December 1, 2010. The plan as always was to have him leave with a bag of cash and return with a bag of pills, but Bowes ended up flying to Florida empty-handed this time.

Just after 2:00 P.M. on Wednesday, December 1, Bowes walked to the corner of Tyler and Harrison Streets in Chinatown where the Chevy Malibu that Colby had rented was parked. Police watched him as he used a key to open the trunk of the car and remove a brown carry-on piece of luggage. Bowes stood on the street corner for about five minutes before Brant Welty rolled up in John's Hummer. Bowes got in and Welty drove them to his house at 21 Wormwood Street in South Boston. They filled the brown bag with $37,500 in cash, and then drove to the airport. A few minutes after Bowes checked in, he was approached by Massachusetts State Police.

"We'd like to talk to you about your luggage," said John Morris, a twenty-year veteran of the State Police force.

"You mean the money in the bag?" Bowes volunteered immediately.

"How much is in there?"

"I don't know," Bowes began. "Maybe thirty thousand dollars. Could be thirty-five or thirty-eight thousand. I'm not sure."

Bowes was taken to a nearby conference room, where he informed the police that he lived in Florida but had come to Boston to attend the funeral of the Nguyen sisters. As the police probed with more questions, Bowes grew visibly nervous. His voice shook and his hands trembled as he stammered a bunch of lies and half-truths. He said he didn't know where he had stayed in Boston, and that he spent most of his time at his sister's house in Nashua, New Hampshire. He said he kept the money in a safe in Boston, but wouldn't say where. He claimed to have made the money working as a bodyguard, but couldn't name a single client. Later in the interview, he said he had come to Boston for a car auction.

"You said you came here for a funeral," Trooper Morris corrected him. "Which is it?"

"Both," Bowes said, doubling down on his lies. "I came for the auction, and then the ladies died."

"So, you came to Boston for the auction, but you stayed in New Hampshire?" Morris asked incredulously.

"Yes."

"You didn't stay anywhere else?"

Bowes must have thought the police had information about where he had stayed because he suddenly blurted: "You mean the Comfort Inn in Dorchester?"

It didn't take much longer to learn that Bowes had also stayed at a friend's house in Dorchester, and while he wouldn't identify John and Anh by name, police knew that's where he had stayed.

The last lie Bowes told the police was that he had come to the airport in a taxi, but police had watched him get out of the Hummer. The troopers could have prolonged Bowes' agony by squeezing the truth out of him, but they already knew the truth. They were simply in the midst of collecting evidence and applying pressure. They seized the money Bowes was carrying and let him board the plane and fly back down to Florida with an empty bag. Bowes didn't object to the seizure of the cash, and he refused the offer to go with the troopers to the barracks where he could get a receipt for the confiscated cash. Once on the plane and out of view of the troopers, Bowes made a phone call to an unidentified person. One minute later, John called Anh.

"Brian got stopped at the airport," John said calmly. "Can you go to the house and make sure the safe is locked?"

"Why?" Anh asked. "What's that got to do with us?"

"What do you mean, 'What does it have to do with us?'" John said with some annoyance. "If he's stupid and doesn't know how to talk, he will tell them he was at my house."

"What does he have on him?" Anh persisted with ambivalence. "Just money, right?"

"Yeah, just money. Just thirty-seven thousand dollars!"

John hung up abruptly. He couldn't be sure that Brian hadn't tipped the police off about himself or even the whole conspiracy. That meant he couldn't go home right away, but he assumed Anh would be safe at the house. She wasn't an active part of the drug scheme, and police wouldn't be after her. He had done his best to keep her ignorant of the inner workings of the conspiracy and to keep her hands clean. Anh was still very much in shock and mourning over the death of her aunts, and John wanted to ease her mind as much as possible. So, he told Colby to go stay at his house with Anh.

"When are you coming home?" Anh asked John in another recorded phone call the next day. "Don't be late. You know I'm gonna be scared."

"Colby's going to wait for you to get home," John reassured her. "All right? He's gonna come late, but he'll show, because he needs thirty-three hundred dollars so he can pay for his fucking apartment."

The plan was for everyone to lie low for a while. John and his coconspirators couldn't be certain why Bowes had been detained at the airport. Maybe the security at check-in just happened to notice an anomaly in Bowes' bag, and they alerted the police; or maybe they had Bowes under surveillance as part of a larger investigation. Either way, things were hot right now, and John told everyone to wait until things cooled down.

Then he was arrested three days later.

John was driving Mark Thompson around Dorchester in his Bentley when a Massachusetts State Trooper noticed the car was missing a front license plate. The trooper stepped up to the driver's side window and asked for John's driver's license and registration. That was a significant problem for John, because the car was registered to Colby Deering, and John didn't have a valid license. Eleven months earlier, John was convicted in Plymouth District Court of operating with a suspended license. He was sentenced to sixty days in prison, but that sentence was suspended for one year. So, as he sat in the car wondering what to tell the trooper, he knew that if he were arrested and found guilty again, he would spend the next two months, including the Christmas holidays, in jail.

"My name is Brant Welty," John lied. "And I don't have my license on me at the moment."

"This isn't your car?" the trooper asked as he perused the registration.

"No, it's my friend Colby's."

The officer called up Brant's driver's license on the computer in the squad car, saw the photo of the real Brant Welty, and quickly discerned that the man in the photo was not the driver of the Bentley he had just stopped. John finally admitted to his true identity, and the officer cited him for operating with a suspended license and arrested him. From the police station, John called Anh and told her what had happened and asked her to come bail him out, which she did.

Back out on the street, John worked some business in between court appearances. He collected a $3,000 debt from a woman named Ah-lung, made additional phone calls down to Florida regarding the pill shipments, and complained to Anh about his current predicament.

"They're looking to put me away," John said. "The judge is a total bitch, and the probation officer is an idiot."

"What are you going to do?" Anh asked sympathetically.

"First, I need another ID," John began. "Then I'm going to run."

"Where will you go?"

"Florida. You and My Linh should come, too. For Christmas!"

John was enthusiastic, but he wasn't pleading. He honestly wanted Anh to join him in Florida, but if she didn't, there were other women down there waiting for him.

"They'll find you in Florida," Anh said flatly.

"I know," John agreed, "but I don't want to spend the holidays in jail. Running buys me some time."

The next day, December 7, John walked into the Wrentham District Courthouse for a pretrial hearing. Before stepping into the courtroom, he made two phone calls, each from a different cell phone. First, he called one of his girlfriends to let her know he would be busy for a while but would call her later. On the second phone, he called Anh and repeated his intention to run if things appeared to be going badly for him. Once inside the courtroom, John listened to lawyers and a judge discuss his future as if they were discussing where to put the family dog during vacation. It was obvious to John that his probation would be revoked, and he would have to serve his sixty-day jail sentence. So, during a short recess, John walked out of the courthouse and didn't return.

Before fleeing to Florida he stopped at Ming Jai's gambling den on Beach Street and sat with Woping Joe at a table. They didn't gamble. They just talked like the old friends they were. John and Woping Joe weren't as close as they had been in the early days of the Chinatown gangs, but John remained indebted to Woping Joe for introducing him to a life and a culture, and for baptizing him into a brotherhood. John still carried the lessons he had learned as a young, incipient gang member as if they were valuable vestiges pressed tightly against his chest. Those core beliefs of loyalty, family, and respect were always close to his heart, and inside his soul. They were his lifeline. They made choosing right from wrong no choice at all. So, before he left for Florida, quite possibly for good, he stopped to say good-bye to his "brother" Woping Joe.

John was telling Woping Joe about what had just happened at the courthouse and what his plans were when one of his cell phones vibrated in his pocket. It was a woman who was actually trying to reach Woping Joe. John handed him the phone and eavesdropped on their conversation in Cantonese. Woping Joe smiled and chatted casually. He appeared smitten with the caller, and that made John smile, too.

"Make sure she doesn't call this number anymore," John advised as Woping Joe returned the phone. "It's time to get rid of it."

A week later, under the delusion that he was safe inside his gated Florida home, John used a new cell phone to make a date with a woman named Frea.

"When are you going to come?" John asked as police listened in. "My wife is still in Boston with our daughter."

With the same phone he told Colby to get "four stacks to that bitch doctor." He was referring to the overdue rent payment of $4,000 to their landlord, who happened to be a doctor.

On the run, up North or down South, it was business as usual for John. Somehow he managed the drug deals, the women, and all the problems that came along with both. After Anh and My Linh came down to Florida for Christmas and New Year's, they returned to Boston so that My Linh could resume school. John stayed in Florida and ramped up the drug operations.

On January 17, 2011, John called Mark Thompson and told him to start gathering pills for a large shipment. Steven

Le, "Little Stevie," was on his way down from Boston with enough cash to buy nearly ten thousand pills. John was on a mission to find and purchase as many as possible. Mark would be able to get at least four thousand pills from Pete Melendez. Thousands more could be procured by Michael Clemente, but there was a sudden glitch.

"I went to see my guys," Clemente told John. "They've upped their price to nine dollars and fifty cents."

"Why the fuck would I pay them that?" John said angrily. "We had an agreed-upon price."

"If you don't pay them," Clemente explained, "somebody else will, and then my guys won't do business with us anymore."

John had always maintained that he didn't care how much money others were making on a deal, as long as he made his, and because he could make his by upping the price on the other end with the consumers, he decided to overlook the disrespect of being strong-armed by the suppliers. He called Clemente back five hours later.

"This dude you're talking with said the other dude is gonna release them, right?" John confirmed. "Is he gonna give them to you now, because I can send him [Little Stevie] now, and get this all done."

"No, I'm on my way back there now," Clemente replied.

"So, what did they have?"

"I'm on my way back to his house right now. I just took whatever he had right then, and now I'm on my way back, and I'm waiting for the guy to come back."

"Okay," Willis said calmly. "My question is what are they gonna have when you get back? Do you know? Because I wanna send as much as I can."

"I'll call you when I get there," Clemente said, hanging up the phone.

Clemente was able to get nine hundred pills from his suppliers, plus a few thousand more from Brian Bowes. Together with the pills Melendez had, the conspiracy was able to secure a grand total of eight thousand pills. John welcomed Little Stevie from Boston, and then told him he had to go right back with the shipment of pills.

"Why do I have to go?" Little Stevie whined. "I just got here. It's fucking freezing up in Boston."

"I'll give you an extra thousand dollars," John bargained. "You can buy yourself a nice winter coat."

Little Stevie agreed to hop back on a plane and return immediately to Boston. He watched Melendez take the pills from zip-locked plastic bags and put them in three large vitamin bottles. Melendez resealed the bottles with superglue and put them in a Walgreen's bag, and then put the bag into Little Stevie's suitcase. It would be the first time Little Stevie transported drugs over state lines.

"Are you down with this?" John asked Little Stevie with some concern. "Are you down, you know, with carrying the pills?"

Little Stevie nodded and headed for the Fort Lauderdale airport. Melendez drove and dropped him off just before 4 P.M. on January 18. Within minutes, Little Stevie was surrounded by deputies from the Broward County Sheriff's office. They were waiting for him.

"Do you mind if we search your luggage?" Sergeant Jeff Paul Cirminiello, a fifteen-year veteran of the Broward County Sheriff's department, asked.

Little Stevie didn't know what to do. His mind raced, and so did his heart. He had trouble focusing. John had always told everyone to cooperate with police if they were ever stopped. That's what John had done. That's what Brian Bowes had done. Of course, both of them were only carrying money. Little Stevie had nearly a quarter of a million dollars worth of narcotics in that suitcase. Still, he consented to the search.

Cirminiello lifted the suitcase onto a table and the muffled, yet distinctive sound of pills rattling could easily be heard.

"Are you transporting pills, Mr. Le?"

"I'm bringing home some 'A thru Z' vitamin pills to my mother," Little Stevie replied.

"Show me."

Little Stevie's hands were shaking and sweating as he pulled out one of the bottles and dutifully opened it up. He spilled several of the pills onto the table, and Cirminiello immediately recognized the tiny blue pills as oxycodone.

"Those aren't mine," Little Stevie blurted.

"They're in your bag."

"I'm just bringing them up for someone else."

Little Stevie knew at that moment he was treading in dangerous territory. He had just told police that he was working with someone else. The logical question would be "Who?"

and the truthful answer could get Little Stevie killed. He decided not to utter another word.

The police counted nearly eight thousand pills, or 929.86 grams, of oxycodone, an amount that carries a street value of at least $240,000. They arrested Little Stevie and held him overnight. John and his coconspirators had no idea anything had happened until the next day, when they began to worry that they hadn't heard from Little Stevie.

"Something's wrong," John told Melendez.

"Maybe it's like what happened to Brian," Melendez said, referring to Bowes. "If they've seen it from the beginning, they were waiting for him to come back, you know?"

"But nobody said nothing," John said. "What are the odds?"

"Listen, John," Melendez said seriously. "I know I took him to the airport, and the fact they didn't grab me, too, may look suspicious, but I swear I had nothing to do with this."

"I know, I know," John said reassuringly. "Don't worry about that. I've just got to figure out how to get dough. I'll go over there to get work started again."

"Work" was among the conspiracy's code words for drugs. John had just lost nearly $80,000 in cash he had used to buy the pills. Without knowing what the bail would be for Little Stevie, he knew there wouldn't be enough money in the Florida house to cover it. He was right. Bail was set at $150,000.

Just as it was done in the old Chinatown days, if someone got arrested, the gang bailed him out. Loyalty was the stated reason, but there was also the reasonable fear that the longer a person is in custody the more likely he is to start talking. John couldn't let that happen.

"We thought he would have killed Steven Le," FBI Special Agent Russell Chisholm would say later, "because of what Le could tell us when he was arrested. He was a courier who could lay the whole thing out for us."

Following Le's arrest, John instructed Colby to grab "five stacks," or $5,000, and bring it down to Florida immediately. He shouted at Colby when Colby said he couldn't get down to Florida until the next day.

"We need the paper!" John shouted, referring to the money.

Colby flew down on the first plane the next morning and met Apponi Malloy at the airport. He brought the money to John, spent less than an hour at the house, and returned to the airport for a flight home.

"Hey, if my girlfriend calls and asks where I was," Colby said to John as he got back in the car with Apponi, "tell her Kevin Baranowski brought me to and from the airport. Otherwise, she'll think I'm with some chick."

Colby had just helped a drug conspiracy launder money and continue its illegal pursuits, but his biggest concern was that his girlfriend might think he was cheating on her.

Little Stevie ended up staying in jail for seven days while the crew found a bail bondsman who would accept $15,000, along with a picture and the title to John's Baja boat. Michael Shaw was called upon to sign the bond, and bail was posted.

Little Stevie, a good soldier who didn't give up any names to the police, was back on the streets with additional charges pending, and John and his crew went right back to work. The only change they made was that they stopped flying the drugs and money back and forth, opting instead to drive up and down the East Coast from Boston to Fort Lauderdale. Of course, the FBI and local police had them all under surveillance. They even had hidden cameras outside the house in Sunrise, Florida, so they could monitor who came and went. Three weeks after Le was bailed out, John and Michael Shaw left Boston headed for Sunrise, but were stopped by police before sunset.

"They've stopped me several times," John says with anger and disdain. "Took a hundred thousand from me one day. I was going to buy a nightclub. They take a hundred thousand, and they write it was dollars for drugs. It was to buy a nightclub. That's one piece of the down payment I was giving the guy who wanted cash."

The day was February 10, 2011, and the precise amount seized was $98,473. John and Michael "Hillbilly" Shaw were traveling in a rented 2011 Chevrolet Tahoe from Boston to Florida on I-95 South when they were stopped by police in Ridgeland, South Carolina. Police maintain it was a routine traffic stop for a lane violation, but it quickly became anything but routine.

Hillbilly Shaw was behind the wheel, and he immediately aroused suspicion when he quite nervously handed over his driver's license. The police officer noticed Shaw's agitation, and then spotted three cell phones in the center console. Those two facts were enough for the officer to begin a more thorough investigation. He asked Shaw to get out of the car and told John to stay in the passenger seat. Shaw proceeded to tell the officer that he and his friend had been snowboarding up in New England for seven days, and were driving back home to Florida.

"Who's that in the car with you?" the officer asked.

"Willis," was all Shaw said.

When it was John's turn to speak with the officer, he identified himself as Brant Welty, and said he didn't have any ID on him.

"We're coming down from New York, where we were just hanging out for a few days," John lied.

The officer went back to Shaw and asked him again what his passenger's last name was, and this time Shaw said he didn't know. It didn't take long for additional officers to arrive, and with what they deemed to be probable cause, they searched the trunk of the car and found a suitcase containing several large bundles of cash wrapped in rubber bands.

"Whose money is this?" an officer asked.

"That's mine," John said.

"Can you tell me how much money this is?" the officer asked John.

"Actually, it's his money," John said, pointing to Shaw. "I knew the money was in the car, but it's not mine."

"So, this is your money?" the officer said to Shaw.

"No."

"Yes, it is," John interjected.

By this time, another officer found another bag with more cash wrapped in rubber bands. It was almost time for John and Hillbilly to come clean, but not quite.

"It's mine," Shaw finally blurted. "I borrowed the money from a friend in Boston. It's about eighty grand. I'm gonna buy a boat."

"Who's the friend you borrowed it from?"

"I don't think I have to answer that."

"No, you certainly don't," the officer concurred. "But without a good explanation of where you got this money, we have the right to presume it's been illegally obtained, and we can take it from you right here, right now."

And that's exactly what the police did. They took the money and let John and Shaw drive away. John was free for the time being, but he was never free from his paranoia.

"You can tell them whatever it's for," John explains. "'I was going to buy a boat.' 'I was going to buy a club.' What's the difference? They're gonna draw their own conclusions, you know? They don't like the fact that here I was, I grew up having nothing. Then all of a sudden, you know I'm driving a hundred-and-fifty-thousand-dollar Mercedes. I'm driving Bentleys. I own a nightclub. I got a liquor store when I'm not supposed to be around any of that, because I have a criminal record. You know, little things that irk the government.

"And then, whether I was doing it, right or wrong— no, something has to be wrong. That's just the way it is. I could've had a dead grandfather who left me a million dollars. It wouldn't have mattered. That's just the way it is with them. I grew up that way. They followed me around. They've been following me around half my life. I don't see how that's legal. I don't see how it's legal, half the things they do. I mean what makes us different than communist China? We are a communist country. But that's fine, you know? My problem with the whole thing is, I'm in a drug conspiracy. You hate me for being part of an organization that extorts, does things our own way or whatever, but yet, the federal government does the same thing."

When John and Shaw were stopped in Ridgeland that day, the truth was that John intended to use the money to complete the purchase of a nightclub called Sky Bar in Fort Lauderdale. A corporation nominally controlled by Brant Welty would have officially been the owner of the club. John's name was never on anything.

About a month after the Ridgeland stop, John was speeding through Dillon, South Carolina, in a black Porsche Cayenne. This time he was driving, and when police pulled him over, he again tried to identify himself as Brant Welty. The problem this time was that the real Brant Welty was sitting right next to him in the passenger seat.

"Both of you guys are Brant Welty?" the officer asked incredulously.

Again, the car was searched and this time police found $42,940 in cash. John told the police the money was Welty's and that it had been earned legally at Welty's liquor store, CRU Wine & Spirits. Welty told the same story, but police seized the money anyway.

"What am I gonna do?" John asks rhetorically. "I wasn't bringing money for drugs. I wasn't doing any of that shit on that trip. But they give you a receipt, a forfeiture notice, and that's it. They don't pull you down to the precinct or anything. They just take your money right on the side of the highway.

You know, it says in the Bible, 'Cast the first stone.' You know? Who's without sin? You know what I mean? They're in conspiracies of their own all the time. Who are they to prosecute me on a conspiracy charge?"

Well, they are the United States government, an imperfect institution to be sure, but one that spent hundreds of thousands of dollars during an eighteen-month investigation, using three to five guys on a surveillance team for each of the people being followed. It was time to cash in on the investment of thousands of man-hours. John Willis and his coconspirators were about to be brought down.

TWELVE

JOHN WILLIS had his shirt off and his feet up. A long night had given way to an early morning, and the bright Florida sun was pouring through the sliding glass door. John had drunk himself to sleep on the living room couch of his Sunrise, Florida, estate, and he was surrounded by empty bottles and glasses as well as several old and new friends who had also chosen to sleep in the very place where they had collapsed. The parties were still good, even if the drug business wasn't.

John put both his hands to his face. He felt the scruff of his beard, then balled his hands into two fists and vigorously rubbed his eyes. He looked like a grumpy four-year-old waking from a nap. Despite his proclivity for crime and his well-established violent past, John possessed soft eyes and a cherubic face. He was boyishly handsome, albeit with a touch of gray around his sideburns. Sitting up slowly, John began to realize his head didn't hurt, and that gave him his morning fix of invincibility. Only someone with omnipotent power can guzzle a bottle of vodka and feel no consequences, he thought. And even though he stood and stumbled and felt a sudden queasiness coming on, he steadfastly maintained that lofty opinion of himself.

The front door squeaked loudly and his good friend Uncle Stevie, an older gentleman uninvolved in the drug conspiracy, burst into the foyer with unexpected anger and energy.

"Do you know you got cameras mounted on the telephone pole outside?" Uncle Stevie asked in a gravelly and robust voice.

"What are you talking about?" John said with quiet alarm.

"You got fucking cameras aimed right at this house," Uncle Stevie explained. "One pointing at the front door and another one pointing at your garage. How long they been there?"

"How am I supposed to know how long they've been there if I didn't even know they were there?"

"Well, you know now. What are you gonna do about it?" Uncle Stevie demanded.

"Nothing," John said, peering cautiously out the window to see the cameras.

"Nothing?"

"Yeah, if they're looking at the front door and the garage, then they haven't seen anything they can use."

"Well, they can see people coming and going," Uncle Stevie said. "And they just got a good look at me!"

Uncle Stevie had walked a couple of miles to the nearest Starbucks for a cup of coffee, and upon his return, he spotted two small boxes mounted on the telephone poles outside John's house. As an ex-con himself, Uncle Stevie was always suspicious and on the lookout. He knew immediately those boxes had nothing to do with the phone lines, but instead contained hidden cameras. He spent several minutes outside trying to figure out where the cameras were aimed, and had concluded his investigation by giving each one of the cameras a big smile and a wave. Uncle Stevie was brash by nature, but his courage in that moment stemmed from the fact that he had nothing to do with John's OxyContin conspiracy.

"I'm outta here," Uncle Stevie declared.

"You can't leave," John protested. "You're my ride."

John was planning to drive back to Boston in two days for My Linh's ninth birthday. Uncle Stevie was scheduled to be the designated driver because John couldn't risk being stopped again by police. John still didn't have a license, but more important, he remained a fugitive from justice relating to his unapproved exodus from the Wrentham District Court five months earlier.

"I'm leaving, and you should, too," Uncle Stevie advised. "Pack a bag, and we'll be outta here in ten minutes."

"Jesus, Stevie! What do you care about a couple of cameras? You've done nothing, and they obviously have nothing on me, or they would have arrested me already. Just calm down, and we'll leave in a couple of days like we planned."

Uncle Stevie was an older man with a burly chest. He was no match for John physically. Not many were. But not many were a match for Uncle Stevie's stubbornness, and his mind was made up. He was leaving with or without John.

"This is bullshit!" John said as he climbed into Uncle Stevie's car and slammed the passenger door. Stevie just smiled and drove out of the garage, stopping to smile once again for the camera.

They were a few hundred miles into their trip when they decided to stop at a diner for lunch. Uncle Stevie took notice of a brown Ford sedan pulling into the parking lot as he and John ate. Stevie was pretty sure he had spotted that same car a few times during their long drive up I-95 North. It kept popping up in his rearview mirror, but never passed them. And now here it was again. The car was still there with two male passengers inside as John paid the cashier and Stevie stepped outside. It gave Stevie a strange feeling, but not enough to initiate a confrontation. He decided to simply make a mental note about the car and drive on. For the next few hundred miles, he checked his mirrors repeatedly and never saw the car again. By the time night had fallen, it was impossible to tell whose headlights were behind him. Still paranoid, but dozing off, Stevie stopped at a cheap motel. Stevie and John shared a room and slept for just a few hours. Early the next morning, they returned to their car, and simultaneously spotted the brown Ford at the far end of the parking lot.

"Son of a bitch!" Uncle Stevie said.

"Ah, who cares?" John replied. "They've been following me my whole life. Let's go."

Without incident, Uncle Stevie arrived in Dorchester around midnight and dropped John off at his home. There was no way of knowing where the brown Ford was, but Stevie was sure it wasn't far away. What he didn't know, and what really bothered him, was whether the Ford would continue following him, or whether John was the target of the investigation. It was the latter.

Bang!

John had barely put his head on the pillow when the first battering ram slammed into the front door at 6:03 in the morning. He had raided the refrigerator when he first got home, and then spent hours watching My Linh and Anh sleep. First, he stood outside My Linh's bedroom, straining in the stillness to hear her breathing. Unable to, he tiptoed like a burglar into her room and lay down next to her. As the digital clock hummed and the minutes passed, John made a lot of plans for what he and My Linh would do together in the weeks ahead. It was already mid-May and school would be out in a month. My Linh would want to get to the beach and to ride her bike around Castle Island in South Boston. The hot dogs and milk shakes at Sullivan's were a summer tradition, and My Linh would be pestering John to take her there soon. He hugged her as any loving, protective father would, but his mind drifted to his recent rash of problems.

The police had stopped him at Logan Airport as far back as October. Brian Bowes was detained in December. Steven Le got pinched in January. And then there were two more stops in South Carolina, and the confiscation of nearly $140,000 in February and March. John didn't worry about the money, because there was so much more of it to be made, both legitimately and otherwise. He also didn't concern himself much with getting caught, because he was almost never around the pills. His misguided thinking was that he couldn't be arrested, and he certainly couldn't be convicted for just having safes full of unaccounted-for cash.

"So, as long as nobody rolls over on me," he thought, "I'll be fine."

Bang!

The sound of the second door ram startled Anh, and she sprang up in bed. She turned and saw John for the first time in weeks. He was calm and his eyes were closed, but she knew he wasn't sleeping. In that moment, she was frightened, and discomfited. The moment she had dreaded and fully expected was finally here, and her shoulders slumped like a beaten fighter between rounds. Then, as if the bell for the next round had sounded, she summoned enough energy and courage to continue the fight. She raced to My Linh's room.

"Don't worry, honey," she shouted, "that's just the police. They're not here to hurt us!"

Like Anh, John instinctively knew it was the police busting through his door, and not some criminal element there to do him harm. So, he was a little slower to rise. He wasn't lifted by the adrenaline rush of fear, nor was he frozen by it. He was more like a concussed fighter trying to make sense of his surroundings and to reestablish reality. Part of his confusion was simply trying to understand his immediate reaction to the banging sounds. Was that relief he was feeling?

"Finally," he thought. "Let's get this over with."

John had a false sense of security regarding his ability to outsmart the feds, but he wasn't delusional about their inevitable and relentless pursuit of him. He and his self-destructive nature knew from the very beginning that the FBI would eventually come after him with the full force of its power. One FBI agent in particular had told him that directly years earlier. So, he wasn't surprised the cameras were outside his home in Florida, or that he had been followed for fifteen hundred miles up the East Coast. And he wasn't distressed by it, either. John was confident the feds had a weak case, and all he had to do was expose that, and maybe they'd go bother somebody else for a while.

By now the police were downstairs shouting, Anh was upstairs screaming, and My Linh was crying. John ran to the top of the stairs and announced he was coming down unarmed.

"I give up," he said with his hands raised. "Just don't hurt my wife and daughter."

Several guns were trained on him as he came down the stairs. When he reached the bottom step, he was instantly grabbed by an FBI agent even larger than himself. John didn't resist, but he grew agitated when the agents rushed up the stairs, guns drawn, looking for anyone else in the house.

"Stop it!" John shouted. "Please, put the guns away. You've got me. My daughter doesn't need to see this!"

Once the agents were satisfied there was no one else in the house and no guns within reach, they assured John that Anh was not being arrested and that My Linh would be okay. John calmed down quickly. He was taken away in handcuffs. Anh and My Linh went to a friend's house, and the FBI agents executed the search warrant.

There were no guns and no pills in the house, but police did find and seize $55,327 in cash and various pieces of expensive jewelry. They also took his 2007 Suzuki motorcycle and the Bentley from his garage. It was while the Bentley was being loaded onto a flatbed truck that Colby Deering came strolling by. He could see the FBI agents in their raid jackets taking boxes out of John's house, but instead of turning around, Colby walked right up to the scene.

"Hey, Colby," one of the FBI agents said casually.

Special Agent Russell Chisholm would later say with a wry smile, "You know it's a bad day when the FBI calls you out by name."

The agents had no intention of arresting Colby that day, and they couldn't force him to speak with them, but Colby inexplicably agreed to be interviewed by the agents inside John's apartment. Sitting at John's kitchen table, Colby told the FBI that he knew John was a drug dealer, and that he was there that day to pick up some money from John. He also admitted to transporting money for John from Massachusetts to Florida several times, and that he used his name to lease property for John. The FBI gleefully took notes as Colby further incriminated himself by stating that he was also the owner of the Bentley in name only, which he may not have realized at the time was an admission of money laundering.

At precisely the same time that John's Dorchester apartment was being raided, a SWAT team from the Miami Police Department swooped in on John's Pompano Beach house.

They came by water and by land. They brought a vehicle designed to ram through the security, but discovered the gate was open. They also discovered Kevin Baranowski passed out on a lounge chair beside the pool. It took a moment to rouse him, but an aggressive nudge from an M-4 rifle did the trick.

Soon after the simultaneous raids in Dorchester and Pompano Beach were complete, the other members of the conspiracy were rounded up without incident. Brant and Bridget Welty, Vinnie Alberico, Aibun Eng, Steven Le, Brian Bowes, Michael Clemente, Michael Shaw, Mark Thompson, and Peter Melendez were all charged in the drug-trafficking conspiracy along with John Willis and Colby Deering. About a week later, Apponi Malloy was added to the list. She was awakened by detectives and members of the FBI at six o'clock on the morning of May 27, 2011, in her North Providence, Rhode Island, apartment and brought to Boston for her arraignment. Police came to get Anh fifteen months later, in August of 2012.

"They rang the doorbell," Anh begins to describe her arrest. "As soon as they rang, I knew it was them. I didn't want to go downstairs. They were decent when they arrested me. They asked me to take off all my jewelry. They allowed me to call My Linh's sitter and to give my neighbor the key to help take care of the dog."

The FBI agents handcuffed Anh and took her to the John Hancock building in Boston to fingerprint and interrogate her. She spent eight hours in a cell, and a few more in a room answering questions. There was very little information she could give them.

"One thing with John," she explains, "he would never, ever put me in any position where I could incriminate myself, but because I've been with him so long, I know enough for them to indict me."

Prosecutors believed they had enough evidence against Anh to prove she was guilty of money laundering, but they wanted more. They convinced a friend of Anh's from a Newbury Street hair salon to call her on the phone and ask specific questions. The feds would record the conversation and hope Anh said something they could use against her or John. The friend's American name is Kevin. In the affidavits for the drug-trafficking conspiracy case, Kevin is never identified. Instead, prosecutors protected his identity and referred to him as John Doe.

"He's a rat!" John says. "This guy turned a simple conversation into a case against Anh. After reading these transcripts of that conversation, it lets people see how corrupt the feds are. That's how they got me to plead out!!"

The story Kevin made up when he called Anh was that his roommate had just sent him a text message saying the FBI had come by his apartment looking for him.

"Oh, they probably were going to ask you about John," Anh said. "Don't go home."

"Perhaps it's about the car," Kevin said, referring to John's Hummer that was in Kevin's name.

"Yeah, if they ask you anything, you tell them you're his friend. That's all. And that you don't know anything. Understand?"

"Yeah."

"If you want, you can come over to my place."

"No, I don't want to go," Kevin said.

"Because talking on the phone, I can't talk on the phone. They often listen on the phone."

Kevin, of course, knew that, because he had consented to having this phone conversation recorded.

"You don't know what he was doing," Anh continued. "It's not a problem. You're just friends with him."

"I didn't do anything," Kevin said. "All of a sudden they came to question me. I was wondering if there's a problem with the car or something."

"There's no problem," Anh assured him. "Already sold the car."

The conversation ended soon thereafter, but at the behest of the FBI, Kevin called back about an hour later. Again, the call was recorded.

"I got home and my roommate said that the FBI agents had asked about the car, the red Hummer. I don't know what to say now."

"You don't need to call them back," Anh barked.

"I thought that the car had been transferred to another person's name. So why did they still ask about it?"

"Who knows? In the past, an FBI agent also came to the house and left his card, but I did not call him back. You don't need to do that."

"How much was the down payment that was paid before?" Kevin asked in a more direct effort to get information for the police about the Hummer.

"Who knows? Do you still have the papers?" Anh wanted to know.

"I don't keep the papers. I don't have any papers at all," Kevin said.

"Just say they have been lost. So you don't have them anymore. You don't need them. After you bought the car, you sold it to people. Because you sold it to people, you don't need to keep the papers. Do you understand? You don't need to call them back."

"I'm very afraid," Kevin lied. "I don't know what to say now."

"What are you afraid of? You were not involved, so you should not be afraid."

Clearly, there were no threats made by Anh, but her statements showed her persistently encouraging Kevin to lie to authorities. She was charged with witness tampering along with money laundering, and eventually pleaded guilty, but served no time.

"Anh was right in the middle of it," Special Agent Chisholm contends. "She was sending money down to Florida. Women in these cases are often tougher than the men. Anh has a federal conviction now. She's not a threat to the community, and is unlikely to start up her own drug dealing operation."

All but one of the principal actors in the conspiracy also pleaded guilty to the charges against them, and based on the severity of their criminal records, received varying sentences.

Brant Welty was sentenced to a hundred months of jail time and three years of supervised release, and ordered to pay a criminal forfeiture money judgment of $85,500.

Bridget Welty received a sentence of time served and a year of supervised release.

Steven Le, who spent over a year in prison awaiting trial, was also given time served and three years of supervised release.

Aibun Eng also was sentenced to time served with a year of supervised release, and a $3,000 fine.

The court imposed a sentence of fifty-seven months in custody for Brian Bowes.

Kevin Baranowski accepted a plea agreement in which he would serve eighty months in jail.

Peter Melendez was sentenced to 160 months in custody.

Michael Clemente got a three-year sentence with a stipulation that he complete a five-hundred-hour drug treatment program.

Apponi Malloy and Michael Shaw cooperated with the investigation and received no jail time. Colby Deering was the only member of the conspiracy to take his case all the way to trial.

"And here's the thing," Assistant U.S. Attorney Timothy Moran said in his closing argument at Colby's trial. "John Willis doesn't get the stuff that makes him want to be a drug dealer. John Willis doesn't get to have the fun of pushing this stuff. He doesn't get the Bentley, or the boat, or the house in Florida without Mr. Deering, without the guy to put a name on it. Without Mr. Deering, there is no drug activity because you don't get the proceeds. That's why it matters. Mr. Deering may not be the drug courier. He may not be the most important person in the drug conspiracy, but here's the thing: If you're in a drug conspiracy, that makes you a drug dealer. That's what he is—a drug conspirator. And here's the thing as well: Even if you're not the guy who drives the Bentley, if you're the guy who knows where the money came from, as he did, and you help out John Willis, that makes you a money launderer."

Colby Deering was sentenced to five years in prison.

As for John Willis, court documents accurately identified him as the kingpin of the conspiracy. With the promise that if he pleaded guilty Anh would not go to jail, he accepted a deal in which he admitted to drug trafficking and money laundering. He was sentenced to twenty years in prison.

"They extort you into signing it," John says of the plea agreement. "You take a guilty plea or whatever it is, because— let's face it—they've got like a 98.5 percent conviction rate. So, they're pretty much telling you, 'I'm giving you a thousand years unless you do this.' It's total bullshit. If you raped a bunch of little kids, they give you less time."

John is serving out his time at the federal prison in Cumberland, Maryland.

"People told on me," John says flatly. "You made your bed. Lie in it. End of story. Discussion's over. I'm not gonna sit here and cry about it. It's over."

The FBI also decided it was over for more than a dozen other subjects of their investigation. On June 30, 2011, Ming Jai, Woping Joe, Hin Pau, and Bai Ming were indicted along with eight others for operating illegal gambling dens and extortion. Wei Xing Chen was charged with another man, Yue Q., with selling Ecstasy and conspiring to induce travel for the purpose of prostitution. Chen, Ming Jai, and Hin Pau received six-, seven-, and eight-year sentences, respectively. Bai Ming got eighteen months.

It was a seven-month investigation that connected John Willis and his codefendants to Chen's brothels and Ming Jai's gambling dens, and it all mushroomed from there as wiretaps and surveillance uncovered the expansive criminal activities of each of the three main targets. When it was over, more than thirty people were arrested and convicted, and authorities seized more than $480,000 in cash and twelve thousand oxycodone pills, along with luxury vehicles and firearms.

Brant Welty also had a gun safe in his South Boston apartment. Included in the safe were firearms he had acquired both legally and illegally. One of the guns, a .40-caliber Smith & Wesson semiautomatic pistol, had been reported stolen from a Stoneham, Massachusetts, residence. And a second gun, a .357 revolver, was reported stolen in Chester, Vermont. Welty also had a Colt Diamondback .38-caliber revolver, a Glock pistol with thirteen rounds of ammunition, a 12-gauge shotgun, a 9mm rifle, more than eight hundred rounds of ammunition, and body armor that had been reported stolen from a federal agent. Furthermore, police seized watches and jewelry from Welty's apartment, including a men's Movado watch and a ladies' gold cluster ring with ten full-cut diamonds.

Also taken in the raids were the red 2005 Hummer H2, the blue 2005 Bentley Coupe, the black 2008 Mercedes E350, the black 2006 Porsche Cayenne, the black 2005 American IronHorse motorcycle, and the 1998 Sea Ray 290 Sundancer that John had named *Double Down*.

"I'm going to make it," John says confidently from inside the Cumberland jail. "This is the truth. I'm not patting myself on the back. Anywhere you put me, I do know how to be a personable human being and understand my environment. I could go out there and find the biggest guy and punch him in the face, have a big fight and decide who's the boss. But what am I the boss of? These stupid trees? All they're going to do is put me in handcuffs and take me to a different prison. That's all they're going to do. What you have to do is adapt to the situation and deal with it. Here, right here, this is where I am. So, what I'm going to do today is I have to deal with it today."

He deals with it by praying, lifting weights, waiting for Anh to visit, and looking back on a life that he's convinced is just and honorable.

"I live a culture that saved my life and took care of me," John explains. "And through my story, through my life, I've been involved in organized crime, which is—it is what it is, you know what I mean? It's not rocket science. I didn't build rockets. I'm not solving cancer, but I am thankful for the culture and the people that I admired, and I live that way."

John acknowledges some, not all, of the crimes he's committed, but he fixates on the loyalty and respect at the core of those crimes so as to rationalize each. He speaks often about a culture, one he was not born into, but a culture generously shared by many and given to one desperate boy crying out for any sense of belonging. He talks reverently about honor, loyalty, and respect, believing each was bestowed upon him with dignity and that he received those gifts with gratitude. He believes that in the absence of those principles, revenge and punishment are justifiable consequences. He avoids the complex contradictions that are inherent whenever prayer precedes extreme violence, and where rules are stringently applied amid chaos. He defends the path he chose because all other paths led to either mortification or demise. John Willis knows who he is, and he claims he is not a gangster.

"My interpretation of me is a person who's about his people," John says, referring to his Chinese brothers. "I grew into a culture, and that's why I feel that my story is not just a gangster story. It's a story of survival. It's a story of camaraderie, and fitting in. My life story goes from when I'm a kid going through my trials and tribulations, my hardships, into a whole new world of organized crime.

"And this is what I can say about my people. If there's certain people involved in gambling, that's what they do. If there are certain people I know involved in prostitution, that's what they do. They're usually the older people that have been involved in this for many years. The younger people, the ones that are coming out, that are in their twenties, they want to involve prostitution with the drug dealing, the drug dealing with the killing. Now these kids today want to be the killer, the drug dealer, the bookie, whatever it is, all in one. So, they basically know a little about a lot of things, instead of knowing a lot about one thing.

"Listen, when I was young, if something had to be done, and somebody had to go away, somebody would come from New York, or California, or Philadelphia, or wherever. They'd come into town for two or three days, do whatever they had to do, and leave. Nowadays, you want to hang out on the corner, and you want to shoot the kid on the same corner, and then expect no one to arrest you. That doesn't happen. Too many cameras. The world has changed. Too many people talk. That's the problem. Times have changed."

THIRTEEN

W HEN JOHN WILLIS wasn't in prison, his ability to function on little or no sleep was an advantage. He could accomplish more and think things through better than his competitors could. He had the time to take care of business, his family, and himself. His days were full, fast, and long. When sunlight's shadows were gone and only the darkness remained, John would find himself alone with only his ever-racing mind to keep him company. And he liked it.

But inside the prison walls, John's days are not full or fast. They are just long. He still doesn't sleep much. So every night, he closes his eyes for what seems like a lifetime while thoughts bounce around inside his head like a pinball. Sometimes it frustrates him, but most of the time, he accepts it as a blessing.

"Right here," he says, tapping his temple. "Sure, they've taken my freedom, but they can't take away what's inside my brain. There are things I can't do, but they can't stop me from thinking."

John looks at the tattoos on his arms. He had chosen the koi fish because it represents wealth and prosperity, and he made sure the artist tattooed the fish swimming toward him, because that meant money would come to him. The dragon was an obvious choice to signify power. And his last tattoo was the Chinese word for pain: *téngtòng*.

"I didn't write the word *pain* on my arm because I felt like every day of my life was a cakewalk," John says with a bit of sarcasm. "There's been pains, and ups and downs, ins and outs, the murders, the life, the loss of life—just the, the different things that go along with this life. But I didn't turn to drugs. I didn't weaken myself. I didn't weaken the structure of my people because of what I was feeling. I did what I had to do, and I'm sorry if some people didn't agree with the things that were done, but that's the way life is. You can't please everybody."

There is still space on John's left arm for more ink. He plans to get additional tattoos, first of his wife and daughter's faces, and eventually of a Chinese warrior. Those images would be accurately reflective of where John's mind and heart are as he counts down his days in prison. He is two parts lonely for his family and one part bitter as hell.

"Do I feel that I'm innocent?" John asks rhetorically. "No. Do I feel I got more time than I should have? Yes. I'm in a cell with a guy who got twenty-seven years. He killed people. Sold drugs. Did whatever. They gave him seven more years than me. I didn't kill nobody. You didn't arrest me for murder. You searched my house over and over. You didn't find one pill. Because I'm in a conspiracy to sell drugs? Twenty years?

"The government has a budget, unlimited time, and they're very much into learning what they can't understand. Me? I'm the guy they couldn't understand. I'm the white kid among a bunch of Chinese and Vietnamese. They're wondering, 'How does this guy fit in?' You know? Then I came up, and I became something where I was making money, buying properties, opening nightclubs. Now it's, 'Whoa, okay. We gotta see what's going on here.' You know what I mean? And that's just the way it is. The federal government is the biggest gang out there. Point blank.

"Do I think that these people are still monitoring my wife because they're still looking for my money?" John asks, and then answers, "Yeah, I think they're still wiring. They're still looking. They're still surveilling. They don't stop. They listen and they watch. They're all about it, y'know?

"I mean, who's the bigger criminal? They are. They're masking it, y'know? Look at communist China. Then look at America. Communist China is doing the same shit as America is doing, but they're out front with it. America— we're being fucked over without the Vaseline, and nobody sees it until it sits on their front doorstep. That's just the way it is. We're no different than communist China or Russia. But it's masked. The criminal entity is within the government. And let's face it: Most criminal entities thrive on cash. This government, the people who run the government, is all about money. And that's just the way it is."

Despite his guilt, and his willingness to unremorsefully admit to most of it, John bristles at how he was caught, believing the wiretaps were unlawfully obtained. He fumes at how he was coerced into pleading guilty to protect Anh from prosecution. And he seethes at the severity of his sentence. Sporadically, he considers those injustices, but he has progressively managed to let go of some of the contributory rage. He makes no effort to do the same as it relates to the colleagues who cooperated with the investigation.

"You go on the street and you do certain things. You tell on people. You take people away from their family. You basically destroy someone's life. You know what's gonna come with that sooner or later. So, you chose to be involved in that. That's what you chose to do. So, that's what you deal with later on."

John's words clearly denote his agitation and anger, but those emotions are conveyed neither in tone nor in body language. He controls the volume of his voice and sits remarkably still. His hands remain folded. Tension in his fingers is undetectable. The degree of his animus needs to be inferred by what he is saying, because he is calculatingly guarded in how he says it. He makes a tireless effort to conceal his anger, perhaps as a self-prescribed strategy to suppress it or simply to offer the pretense that he is more cultivated than one would expect a violent criminal to be.

"Love is the most powerful emotion," he says unexpect-edly. Then as if his listener would assume otherwise, he adds, "It's not anger. If you've got someone who truly loves you and you love them, you'll do anything for them. Anger stops. It's a reaction."

John Willis, of course, knows much more about anger than love. He was angry as an abandoned teen, and he's angry as an isolated and imprisoned middle-aged man. His anger never did stop, and it wasn't merely a reaction. No, for John Willis, anger was at the root of his survival. He used it to fuel his desire, to cross lines of moral ambiguity, and worse. Anger had filled his heart and served him well for many years. Anger had helped him avoid pain. Love only caused it.

"My mom and Anh were the only real love I've ever felt," he says. "Real love comes when you go through hardships, and you deal with them, and then it's where you are with that person. There's a lot of pain."

John is at first stoic as he espouses his rather cynical view of love, and then smiles at the absurdity of something so wonderful also being so fraught with danger. And then his eyes begin to well up with tears.

"It's torture," he says, weeping suddenly. "I think every day away from my daughter, my wife, is more painful. You think you'd get used to it, but it's not something that anyone tries to get used to."

John's round face turns red and he jams two thumbs into his eyes to block the tears from rolling down his face. He looks up at the ceiling, the tears pooling and blurring his vision.

"I got this advice from a friend of mine," he continues. "He's a hit man for the Italians in New Jersey. He said, 'John, don't be anything to My Linh but a friend.' He tells me I'm not in a position to tell her what to do. I'm in a position to listen. So, I try to understand, but I can't guide somebody from where I'm at. That's the hardest thing even with Anh, because you're not who you are when you're outside these walls. How do you get somebody to hear you from seven hundred miles away?"

John speaks with a quivering voice, showing a vulnerability not many have ever witnessed. He rubs his hands roughly over his face, sniffles deeply, and exhales in a short burst. A moment later, it is clear he has regained his composure and can continue.

"I look at what's important," he says. "What's important is my daughter and my wife. If I can get a phone call and make sure that they're good, and they're fine, then my day's great. When I lay my head down at night and I know they're home, they're safe, everything's good, that's another day gone. Every day that I sit here still counts. It's closer to whatever day they decide they wanna ever let me go home. You know, it's a day closer to getting closer to my wife, and my family, and being back out there."

He finishes the thought with a resoluteness that suggests strength and perseverance will follow, but once again, and with equal suddenness, he begins to cry. His eyes fill up with tears and he blurts: "The scariest thing for me in my life is losing my family: Anh leaving or being with somebody else. I've never been insecure in my life, but I'm sitting in here now. Is she going to be there? I have never felt like a piece of shit with my brothers, but I have felt that way with Anh, like I have not been the man I wanted to be, like I let her down. I think about that a lot. There's nobody else in my life who deserves the time it takes me to look at my shortcomings. She's been through a lot with me. Nobody in this world knows me better than Anh. I've been deceitful and lying. I've been open. I've been closed. She can look at me and tell if I'm telling the truth."

John is tired. He sits back in his chair and closes his eyes. He has experienced much pain in his life, but none greater than what he feels at this moment. He misses his wife and daughter. He fears for their safety, and his helplessness is agony. It seems his heart, so full of anger, has just enough room for genuine love, because it is breaking.

"Everybody wants the underdog to come through," John says, wiping his eyes. "Everybody wants to see the story of survival. Nobody wants to live the pain, but they want to share the story."

And as John Willis shares his story, he tries to give the impression that he is opening himself up completely, because he wants desperately to be understood, but because he only opens himself up partially, it becomes obvious that his purposefully chosen words and disciplined mannerisms are an extension of his need to control and manipulate others. It's quite possible he doesn't want so much to be understood as to be forgiven, and to that end, he engages in a continuous attempt to persuade.

"I think I did the right things for the right reasons," he contends. "That's why I did what I did. This part of my life is more about the pain, the struggle that we all go through. Survival is what we all do every day, you know what I mean? So for me, this story is about the struggle of not having parents, the struggle of, you know, having to prove yourself on a daily basis, to learn a culture. You know, to live in a time where there wasn't really conversation. Today, you get in a fight, you tell a guy, you know, 'I'm gonna get you.' If you said that twenty years ago, you were dead. Somebody came to kill you. Nobody gave you the chance to get them."

John is a little more animated now. He never had his day in court, so he treats any conversation about his life like he is a defendant on the stand. He is pleading—not for mercy, not for justice, but for the slightest amount of sympathy. *Put yourself in my shoes*, he seems to say, *and you might have also done what was required to survive.*

"The way I lived and how I think it all started from here," John says, pointing to his brain. "You have to start from here," he says, again tapping his temple, "and this is how I learned, and where I learned, and the way I thought, and the way my perceptions of things became. As a kid, I was fun and games. Then real life happened. Cut the fun and games out. I was young. After the fun and games were out, it's what are we going to do to survive in the real world. Next thing, I'm involved with some very serious people. If I don't adapt or understand what's going on around me, I might not make it."

There is, of course, respect for John's intellect. He is thoughtful, measured, and eloquent. He is a highly proficient problem solver. He is also physically powerful, but his muscle would be impotent without his mind, and he's smart enough, self-aware enough, and arrogant enough to realize that.

There is, of course, empathy for a boy who was abandoned by his father, and who watched his mother slowly die. And there is, of course, compassion for a man looking at twenty years separated from the woman and child he loves.

But, of course, the respect, empathy, and compassion are mitigated by the fact that John Willis is a violent criminal, and that he has deluded himself into thinking he did only what he had to do to survive. John points to his early struggles and the tragic circumstances that initiated his transformation from a starving teenager in Dorchester to a high-ranking leader of a Chinatown gang, but he scoffs at the notion that he could have struggled like an ordinary person, waiting tables, working construction, or driving a bus. He wanted an easier life of women, cars, boats, and gambling. Selling drugs—first marijuana and coke, and then OxyContin—was his pathway to that life. When he says, "I always knew I'd end up in jail or in a grave," he says it with hints of both apathy and bravado.

"From the day we took our first crawl to our first job," he analyzes, "we took strides and steps to become a better human being, a more efficient human being. So now here I am, years later, I'm forty-two years old. I've been through murders, wars, the goods, the bads, whatever, but through every experience we have in life, we take something from that.

"This is not a drug dealer story. It's the story of a culture. It's a way of life, an organization, you know? Meaningful stuff. Meaningful, like camaraderie, brotherhood, you know, an acceptance. I don't think white people anywhere in the Asian culture are accepted the way I was or am. And for me, I'm grateful for that. I'm always going to be who I'm gonna be. I'm always going to have the same goals, to take care of my family and my daughter, to not change who I am as a human being, to have honor. Honor and respect, that's all that people want in their life. No matter how they get it."

John Willis wants people to see him as good and honorable and loyal, and to see his actions as justified, and ultimately to disregard all evidence to the contrary. This is why he remains offended by the sobriquet "White Devil."

"If you look at Chinese people," he explains, "they're not going to say, 'Oh John, he's a white devil.' They're going to say, 'He's Bak Gui John.' *Bak gui* is like 'white ghost.' My Chinese name is 'Loong Jai.' *Loong* is 'dragon.' The reason they call me dragon is because I was bigger and stronger. So, it's a show of power. So Bak Loong would be like 'White Dragon,' you know what I mean? The feds came up with 'White Devil' to make me sound like this inhumane person, you know. I've read all the terrible things they've written about me. They put on the Internet that I'm the White Devil, this terrible devil. That's not what it means. The White Devil? Who the hell is the White Devil?"

Indeed.

ACKNOWLEDGMENTS

WRITING IS BOTH a lonely and fulfilling endeavor. So much of it is done in the solitude of a small upstairs office or in a quiet room at the library. Even at a crowded Starbucks or in the company of others, a writer can get lost in his own thoughts and escape into his own world, because when you're writing a book, you're always writing that book. It's never very far from your mind.

So, I'd like to start by thanking my wife, Eileen, a fabulous writer herself, for understanding the moodiness that comes with being blocked, the disappointment of an unproductive day, the frustration of recognizing flawed or confusing writing, and the stress involved in undertaking a massive project and attempting to successfully meet deadlines. Thank you. We made it through another one!

My kids also get a little less of me when I'm writing. So, thank you, Sean, Dan, Liam, and Grace for letting me pursue a passion without complaint. I love you all!

This book never would have been written without the incredible work of my manager, Matt Valentinas. Once he sold John Willis' story to a movie studio, he could have asked anyone to write the book, and publishers would have been interested. He chose me—first, I think—and provided me with a great opportunity to learn about and tell a fascinating story.

My editor, Erin Kelley, was a pleasure to work with. Writers can fall in love with their own words, but like a good friend, Erin would wisely let me know which words I needed to break up with. Her attention to detail, her ability to streamline the story, to make it more conversational, more intelligent, and less confusing, was not only needed but greatly appreciated. If you knew how this book was first handed in, and compared it to its final version, you'd thank Erin as well.

I'd like to thank John Willis' cousin Debbie for providing context and perspective to John's childhood; FBI Special Agent Russell Chisholm for his time and insight, and for explaining how the case against John initially began and was successfully investigated; and David Yee, who volunteered information about his own criminal past, and helped me better understand John's motivations, loyalties, and passions.

Obviously, very special thanks and gratitude go out to John Willis and Anh Nguyen. They were each willing to tell their story honestly without hubris or humility. They gave me their time. They gave up their privacy. And I believe they will give readers a unique, and possibly important, look at a world that has never been opened up like this before. Readers will no doubt see John and Anh as greedy, manipulative, and opportunistic criminals—all of which is revealed in their own accounts of their lives. But they were equally candid about their love story. And I thank them for that, because unwittingly, I believe, they provided a context that humanizes the story's main character, John Willis, and that makes for a more compelling read.

ABOUT THE AUTHOR

BOB HALLORAN is an award-winning broadcast journalist currently working as a news and sports anchor at WCVB-TV in Boston. He has authored six books, including *Irish Thunder*, *Breakdown*, and *Impact Statement*. He is married to the wonderfully loving and generous Eileen Curran and is the exceptionally proud father of Sean, Dan, Liam, and Grace. If he had a bumper sticker, a gravestone, or a tattoo, they would all read: "I'd rather be golfing!"